The task of making disciples is increasingly capturing the church. George Miley in *Maturing toward Wholeness in the Inner Life* approaches this work from the view that following Jesus requires a Christ-formed inner life. The Lordship of Christ emerges from transformations within. Fr. Miley patiently builds a case, chapter by chapter, providing the necessary tools through pithy phrases or "tweet-length" statements. In our mad-dash world, a seeker after Christ, or even a mature disciple, can pick up this book and take a small step toward Christ-likeness even with only a few moments available to read. This book is versatile, honest, clear and impactful. I commend it to you!

— *Rt. Rev. Keith Andrews, Bishop of the Diocese of Western Anglicans,*
Anglican Church in North America

In *Maturing toward Wholeness in the Inner Life,* George Miley shares the fruit his years of spiritual formation, engagement with the breadth of the Christian tradition, and his experience working with Christian leaders around the world in pithy yet profound tweets. George's characteristic gentleness, depth, and clarity are on display throughout each chapter. The book is a call and an invitation into a deeper life with God, a deeper relationship to the body of Christ, and a deeper love for the broken world that God is restoring to beauty through the gracious, Spirit-infused practices so compellingly articulated in these pages.

— *Rev. Chris Schutte, Rector, All Saints Anglican Church, Durham, NC*

This book is a profound gift that will take the reader on a journey that is both fresh and wonderfully accessible. George Miley is someone who has walked deeply with God and the fruits of this rich relationship are the wisdom and insight into what it looks like to live intimately with Jesus. This book has been transformational for me as a husband, father and leader, as I trust it will be for you as well.

— *Ryan Thurman, International Director, Antioch Network*

God invites his people into new life, a life in His Kingdom. But what does that look like? George Miley has thought deeply about that question and has years of experience working with believers around the world. The insights and reflections God has given him are captured in this short but powerful book. I encourage anyone who is hungry to experience and express the Kingdom of God in your life to join George in the life-long journey of discipleship to Jesus.

— *Shawn Carson, Lay leader, Christ Church Anglican, Phoenix, AZ*

The short statements in this book guide the reader into the very essence of discipleship. By meditating, digesting and practically living these texts my life has been changed—especially my "every-day-ordinary" life with my constant struggle between practical and spiritual responsibilities. George re-introduced into my days the secret of a rhythm of prayer and work—ancient monastic wisdom I had left behind because I chased the freedom of the Spirit. Now these rhythms bring order to my days and impulses for prayer into my occupation. This book will also be a very helpful guide for groups seeking to grow in faith together. The short but dense texts go deep. I recommend to "eat" this work in small portions. You will, like me, come out satisfied, healed, calm and serene.

— Dr. Gabriela Schubert, leadership team, Mercy House of Prayer Vienna, Austria

Drawing from powerful personal life experiences, George Miley, in this well written book challenges us to deeper spiritual growth, soul care… becoming Christlike and more. Read this book – every tweet is a nugget, every sentence draws us into conversation with self and God.

— Lawrence Tong, DD., International Director, Operation Mobilization

Surely every follower of Jesus Christ wants to live a life pleasing to God. In this book George Miley draws from his own experience over many decades in serving God in different ministries as well as the saints of God through history. The aim of this book is to challenge the reader to pursue a life that will have an impact in the world and glorify God. It is practical and inspiring and a very helpful tool for every Christian.

— Manfred Schaller, Chairman of the Board (Emeritus), OM Ships International, and Prädikant in the Protestant Church of Baden, Germany

This book is a compelling read because George Miley is authentic, writing only what he has gleaned from meditation, reflection, and gained from life's experiences. George has lived his life exemplifying all that he expounds in the 24 chapters of the book. A testament to his life that speaks volumes to me, is how he has demonstrated Christ's love for the church, by loving his wife Hanna so deeply, to walk with her through a sad and tragic past to the present, of restoration and reconciliation.

The content of this book has substance, and gives you practical insights to spiritual maturity in bite-sized pieces, which makes it easy to read and to extract a personal lesson to act upon. George has crystallized the spiritual gems found in this book, what must have been through precious seasons of discipline, meditation, revelation and learning, and shared them with us so generously. I highly recommend this book and it will join the section called 'Classics' in my library.

— Mrs. Belinda Liok-Tay, fourth generation Singaporean Christian and granddaughter of Faithful Luke, a co-worker with Watchman Nee in China

In the tradition, on the one hand, of the short, pithy sayings of the desert fathers and, on the other, contemporary masters like Willard, Foster, and Nouwen, George Miley has gifted those who seek maturity in Christ with a map. I believe this genre is ideal for active meditation but also allows space for God to work in our hearts. I highly recommend *Maturing toward Wholeness in the Inner Life*.

— *Dr. John DelHousaye, Prof. New Testament & Spiritual Formation, Phx Seminary*

In 2010 George Miley led a five day retreat for our community, Christ the Reconciler, in which he presented several teachings on inner healing, spiritual disciplines and growth toward maturity in Christ. These teachings, now compiled and expanded in *Maturing toward Wholeness in the Inner Life*, were significant in transforming both individual lives and our community as a whole. The simple, unadorned statements in this book leave space for contemplation and direct dialogue with the Holy Spirit. We are thankful that this teaching which has blessed us so deeply is now available to many others in the Body of Christ.

— *Thomas and Amy Cogdell, Founders, Christ the Reconciler, Elgin, TX*

Just as Jesus taught his disciples and allowed them to participate in his life, so today more than ever it is crucial that Christians mature spiritually and emotionally, and are transformed toward becoming increasingly like Christ. The author gives wonderful guidance for experiencing this. The book is especially recommended for Christian leaders.

— *Verena & Hans-Peter Lang, Austrian Round Table,*
An Initiative for Unity in the Body of Christ

In *Maturing toward Wholeness in the Inner Life*, George Miley teaches us with direct and accessible language about living in God's Presence and how transformed lives manifest God's kingdom. George's book is beautifully written and presented, offering spiritual and practical nourishment. As a companion book, I'll return often to *Maturing toward Wholeness in the Inner Life* for contemplation and encouragement. Thank you George for this important book.

— *Jim Craft, General Counsel, Apogee Physicians*

I have learned so much from George and Hanna Miley, and this book is like having them with me as the mentors and friends they have for so long been. Maturing Towards Wholeness in The inner Life is a treasure chest of wisdom for spiritual formation, maturity and leadership. The manner in which George brings us his insights and wisdom is worth a careful read, and regular and ongoing quiet contemplation.

— *John Kelly, President, Kelly Benefit Strategies, Kelly & Associates Insurance Group*

We desire to sit at the feet of people who have proven their followership of Jesus through authentic kingdom living. We hope they write a book (don't we?) about this accumulated wisdom from decades of this apprenticeship. George Miley is that mature leader who has done just this, choosing a novel proverbial way of communicating a lifetime of wisdom, delivering it ... twitter-fashion. This isn't a book to read cover to cover at the beach, it is instead a mighty meal intended to be eaten one tweet at a time.

— *Dr. Kit Danley, President, Neighborhood Ministries, Phoenix, AZ*

A brilliant way to capture fundamental truth about the journey our Lord takes us on. George, presents on these pages through reality of life, the awesomeness of God through His word. God is restoring us to Himself each day and this book is a tremendous encouragement along this journey.

— *Seelan Govender, CEO, OM Ships International*

"You are looking at the wrong person," is a foundational statement of George Miley that has shaped our friendship for 12 years. Looking at ourselves or others (looking at the wrong person) traps us in our daily problems. George communicates the life-transforming power of looking only to God, listening to his Word, and waiting for him to act. Through this book God speaks directly into our lives with irrefutable truth and love. Whoever seeks deep and lasting change through God's grace should read this wonderfully understandable book.

— *Dodo Benecke, Prädikantin in the Lutheran Protestant Church of Bavaria*
— *Hubertus Benecke, Attorney, Benecke Rechtsanwälte, Oberfranken, Germany*

Maturing toward Wholeness in the Inner Life has sent us on a wonderful path to explore and discover more of God's plan, vision, and purpose for our lives. George Miley has a profound gift of unwrapping biblical truths and enlightening human paths. His simple but deep and short Tweets (statements) are a pleasure to read time and time again.

— *Ludwig Benecke, Attorney, Benecke Rechtsanwälte, Oberfranken, Germany*
— *Cecily Benecke, Staff at Quellen*

George Miley has distilled the wisdom of nearly a lifetime of walking with God into an accessible guidebook. Practical and profound, George's presentations of God's truths are helpful for any reader at any point in a spiritual journey. I'm thankful to have this resource for addressing important questions written in such an approachable style.

— *Phil Thomas, Owner, Chick-fil-A Restaurant, Phoenix, AZ*

Finally a book about how life with Jesus really works. Finally a book from convincing examples in faith. Finally a book written by a married couple. Finally a book that answers where we are going, sustainable and into the next generation. It is full of true reconciliation, fellowship, with godly principles. As a businessman I like a lot that it talks about a building up of local movements, as all business is local. Finally a book that explains how local fellowship can work. Finally a way in which a local fellowship can enter a network and be taught how networking may work. So true, so right, so credible.

— *Prince Michael zu Salm-Salm, Entrepreneur, Wallhausen, Germany*

George Miley is a gifted and insightful writer, teacher, preacher, scholar and leader. I have been personally blessed for many years by his uncanny ability to distill complex spiritual and theological themes into simple, understandable, and poetically beautiful messages. I have heard it said in our bustling and industrious lives we often find we are drowning in information but starved for knowledge. I am confident that busy readers of *Maturing toward Wholeness in the Inner Life* will benefit from George's method and style and will–a few words at a time–discover profound understandings rooted in the teachings of Jesus.

— *Michael Hunter, Chief of Staff to Speaker of the Arizona House of Representatives*

For both the purposes of private devotion and times of collective retreat, *Maturing toward Wholeness In the Inner Life*, is a thought-provoking and grace-filled foundation for growth into Christian maturity. This collection of wisdom drawn from Scripture and a life of discipleship is a wonderful resource for learning how to grow in Christ, and a gift for the Church as it seeks to follow after Jesus Christ today. Thanks so much, George, for the book, the retreat, and all that you and Hanna mean to us at Christ Church Anglican.

— *Rev. Matt Rucker, Priest in Charge, Christ Church Anglican, Phoenix, AZ*

I have gone through this entire book and now its message is going through me. This is not an evangelical snack, but a spiritual feast. I will want to go back to it and use it especially in my quiet and devotional time. I have known George and Hanna for over half a century and know they WALK THE TALK, that ministers to me as much as the book.

— *George Verwer, Founder, Operation Mobilization International*

ABOUT THE AUTHOR

In *Maturing toward Wholeness in the Inner Life*, George Miley draws on over five decades of Christian ministry experience as a local church pastor, cross-cultural pioneer, mission leader, mentor and friend. His wife Hanna is Jewish, born in Germany, and escaped the Holocaust alone as a 7 year old in 1939. Her parents died in the death camp in Chelmno, Poland, on May 3, 1942. The Mileys are engaged in a ministry of discipleship, reconciliation, mentoring, teaching, and writing, based both in Germany and the US.

FURTHER WORKS

by George Miley

Loving the Church… Blessing the Nations:
Pursuing the Role of Local Churches in Global Mission

by Hanna Zack Miley

A Garland for Ashes:
World War II, the Holocaust, and One Jewish Survivor's
Long Journey to Forgiveness

Meine Krone in der Asche:
Der Holocaust, die Kraft der Vergebung und der lange
Weg zur persönlichen Heilung

More resources available at Quellen.Org

Maturing toward Wholeness in the Inner Life

George Miley

ISBN: 978-0-578-61371-0

Editorial team: Hanna Miley, Cheri Beckenhauer,
Ludwig Benecke, Matt Rucker
Book design and cover: Cheri Beckenhauer

First Edition

Published by Quellen
https://quellen.org

DEDICATION

Maturing toward Wholeness in the Inner Life has been written for younger followers of Jesus the Messiah who are coming after us in the faith, and with whom the Holy Spirit has united us in deep affection. I am thinking especially of Hubertus, Dodo, Thomas, Amy, Ryan, Noleen, Ludwig, Cecily, Jess, Cheri— along with others.

You are the ones who in God have called forth this writing. This book would not have been written except that you, in so many gentle ways, have asked for it. Affection for you has given the energy to write during a season of "old age and gray hairs" (Psalm 71:18), when strength has been noticeably receding.

Maturing toward Wholeness in the Inner Life is an expression (inadequate) of the life which we, by His grace, share with God. It is written as an offering to him. If you discover anything of value here, it is a gift of his grace—first to us, now to you.

I have learned more about God from Hanna than from any other person—no one else comes close. There is no teaching I could give that is not permeated with her insight. As a life partner, God has given me a modern-day prophetess of Israel.

We bless you in the name of Yeshua, the Messiah of Israel, the Lord of the Gentiles, the Savior of the world, the coming King.

George, with Hanna

> Hear, O sons [and daughters], a father's instruction,
>   and be attentive, that you may gain insight....
>
> The beginning of wisdom is this: Get wisdom,
>   and whatever you get, get insight.
>
> Prize her highly, and she will exalt you;
>   she will honor you if you embrace her.
>
> She will place on your head a graceful garland;
>   she will bestow on you a beautiful crown.

Proverbs 4:1,7-9

CONTENTS

Preface: *Why Is George Writing in Tweets?* i

Overview: *The Original 40 Tweets?* iii

1 **Restore the Ancient Anointings** 1
Elijah Was a Man with a Nature like Ours

2 **Discipleship** 12
Becoming Able to Live the Way Jesus Said Was Best

3 **Humility** 16
Living with What Is True About God and Me

4 **The Kingdom of God** 20
Unseen Reality

5 **Practicing God's Presence** 24
Where I Am Re-Formed

6 **Faith** 28
Choosing to Rely on God for Forgiveness of Sin and Everything Else

7 **Inner Healing** 33
Healing the Pain That Is Blocking My Maturing

8 **Spiritual Practices** 38
Exercises for Inviting God's Healing Presence into My Inner Life

9 **Solitude** 43
Ushering My Soul into the Healing Silences of God

10 **How to Spend Time in Solitude** 47
A Day, or Hours, or Minutes

11 **Prayer** 50
Being with God and Interacting with Him about All We Are Doing Together

12   Prayers That Can Be Prayed in Five Seconds   55
      Toward moment by Moment Communion

13   With All Your Heart   59
      Create in me a clean heart, O God, and renew
      a right spirit within me. Psalm 51:10

14   With All Your Soul   64
      The LORD is my shepherd; he restores my soul. Psalm 23:1,3

15   With All Your Mind–Thoughts   71
      May the mind of Christ, my Savior, grow in me from day to day,
      by his love and power transforming all I do and say.

16   With All Your Mind–Emotions   77
      The fruit of the Spirit is love, joy, peace, patience, kindness, goodness,
      faithfulness, gentleness, self-control. Galatians 5:22-23a

17   With All Your Strength – The Body   85
      Your body is a temple of the Holy Spirit. You are not your own.
      So glorify God in your body. 1 Corinthians 6:19-20

18   Loving Your Neighbor (Personal Relationships)   91
      Above all these put on love, which binds everything together
      in perfect harmony. Colossians 3:14

19   Sexuality   98
      God's Gift for Physically Expressing "One-of-a-Kind" Intimacy

20   Learning How to Forgive   105
      Changing the Effects of the Past on the Present and the Future

21   The Ministry of Reconciliation   110
      Bringing Healing and Beauty to Wounded Relationships

22   Honor Your Father and Mother   116
      Learning God's Ways in Relating to Authority

23   *New Life Comes Forth from Death*   123
      It Is No Longer I Who Live but Christ Who Lives in Me

24   Grace   131
      God Doing for Me What I Cannot Do for Myself

My hope is to gain a fresh hearing for Jesus, especially among those who believe they already understand him. In his case, quite frankly, presumed familiarity has led to unfamiliarity, unfamiliarity has led to contempt, and contempt has led to profound ignorance.

— Dallas Willard, from the Introduction to *The Divine Conspiracy*

Why Is George Writing in Tweets?

Many words generate trivial words.
Trivial words obscure insight, dilute wisdom.

I too was surprised to find myself beginning to write this book in tweets. What brought me to do this? It was a journey that I backed into.

For Christmas 1998 my mother gave me Dallas Willard's *The Divine Conspiracy.* I started reading. Half-way through I began to make notes in the margins. Then I began to underline. My next thought was: "I need to read this book again." I read that copy of *The Divine Conspiracy* five times. I made more notes. I underlined. The spine broke. I still have the book on my shelf.

I have gone through seasons of life when I thought wisdom was to try to read as many books as possible. And I have read a lot of books. *The Divine Conspiracy* changed all that. Here was something deep— enduring. It would be treasured long after most books had gone out of print. It transformed my orientation.

Now I wanted to unearth the author's thought processes. How did he arrive at his understandings? What was the essence, the core insights, the conceptual foundations? I began slowly to key the entire book into a word processing document. It took me a year. I was in no hurry. I did a couple of pages a day during my early morning study times. I highlighted the key insights. I deleted all explanatory material surrounding each key insight. I bolded the most important phrase in each one. I gave them each a number. I kept going over the key insights during my morning study times. Understandings took root in my subconscious. A study method was emerging.

I studied other authors this way—Leanne Payne, Dietrich Bonhoeffer, Richard Foster, the Desert Fathers, Robert Webber, Henri Nouwen, et. al. My study was transitioning from reading widely to meditating deeply. I focused on classics—writings that have endured the test of time. I was on a hunt for essence. What are foundational understandings upon which a house of wisdom can be built that will survive and flourish? I knew such understandings must be expressed in few words and, rooted in the concepts of Jesus, the greatest Teacher ever to live.

Our 21st century lives are submerged in a tsunami of words. Many words generate trivial words. Trivial words obscure insight, dilute wisdom. Just prior to starting this book our co-worker Cheri assigned me the job of writing 40 tweets to post on twitter, Facebook, and our website. Creating 40 tweets felt like writing poetry. This had become my style! I would write *Maturing toward Wholeness in the Inner Life* in tweets.

The Original 40 Tweets

1. A state governor, an evangelical Christian, was exposed in a very public extra-marital affair. What causes such breakdowns—when behavior contradicts Christian confession?

2. Jesus spoke of another kind of life, different to what humans typically experience—one permeated with meaning, fulfillment, integrity, joy.

3. Jesus made astounding claims about the life he offers. It is like water to the thirsty, bread to the hungry. It is life in abundance.

4. The life Jesus described was eternal in quality as well as duration. He came to restore to humans the ability to share God's life with him.

5. Jesus: "This is eternal life, that they know you the only true God and Jesus Christ whom you have sent" (Jn. 17:3). Eternal life is knowing God.

6. What was Jesus talking about? To many he seemed out of touch with the "real world." But Jesus was speaking about a deeper, Unseen Reality.

7. Jesus said the life he came to bring is not found by searching the human ideas and traditions all around us. It comes from another Source.

8. Jesus spoke about the kingdom of God—the sphere in which God rules. This was the central subject in his teaching. He said it was "at hand."

9. Jesus said the kingdom of God (of heaven) is available to all, right now, here, next to us, all around us. And it is profoundly desirable.

10. Jesus said the kingdom of heaven is like treasure hidden in a field, which a man found, sold all he had, and bought the field (Mt. 13:44). Smart man!

11. Who was this Jesus who was making such claims? Where did he get his information? People said he spoke with authority. "No one ever spoke like this," they said.

12. If God's unseen Kingdom is open to everybody, right now, two questions arise:
    • How does one enter?
    • Once in, how does one live there?

13. Jesus said we enter God's Kingdom:
    • by choosing to turn from our old ways (repentance) and
    • by relying on him (faith)
    • He is the door in.

14. Entering God's kingdom, we come into his Presence—the most fulfilling, life-giving experience we have ever had. We want to remain there 24/7.

15. But we quickly find that to come free from our old ways takes more than willpower. Many of our old ways are deeply entrenched destructive habits.

16. We try hard to change. We rely on our own strength. Our own strength fails us. We ultimately fall back into discouragement, failure, quiet desperation.

17. A tragic misunderstanding among Christians: Teach someone how he should behave, and willpower will enable him to do it. The failures are all around us.

18. It is widely assumed that the Christian life will be characterized by failure. Can this be because so many only experience failure? Is this really what Jesus and the apostles taught?

19. Inability to live God's ways in our own strength brings us to the second question: How does one learn to live with God in his kingdom?

20. We live in God's kingdom the same way we entered—we turn from our own ways and rely upon Jesus in all of life. But we need to be re-formed (transformed) to be able to do that.

21. Jesus is known as Savior and Lord. We must also come to know him as Teacher. "You call me Teacher and Lord, and you are right, for so I am" (Jn. 13:13).

22. Having announced that God's kingdom is now available to all, Jesus called disciples. In discipleship he taught them the ways of God's rule.

23. We can understand discipleship with Jesus as being an apprenticeship. In an apprenticeship we have:
    • A master
    • Apprentices (learners)
    • Skills to be mastered

24. In discipleship with Jesus:
    - Jesus is the Master
    - We are the apprentices (learners)
    - The skills to be learned are how to live in God's kingdom

25. Much Christian teaching tells me how I ought to behave. But behavior is largely an expression of character—the person I have become on the inside.

26. What I really need to know is how character is re-formed—how the inner life can be re-shaped toward Christlikeness. Jesus knows how.

27. To change behavior, Jesus did not focus on behavior. He focused on transforming character—the inner life. He said to grow good fruit you need a good tree.

28. On the cross Jesus forgave his killers. How did he do it? Superhuman willpower? Or was he just the kind of person who forgives his enemies?

29. In the Sermon on the Mount Jesus was not moralizing, but describing. Describing what? How people behave who have hearts re-formed in the righteousness of God's kingdom.

30. God's ways become my ways as Christlikeness is gradually formed in me. I become the kind of person, for example, who prefers forgiveness to bitterness.

31. Living in God's kingdom is living under God's rule. Living under God's rule is living in God's Presence. In God's Presence I am

    gradually changed.

32. God created me for his Presence like he created fish for water. God's Presence is my true home. Why then do I find staying there so hard?

33. Barriers within me hinder or block me from abiding in God's Presence. For example:
    - guilt
    - deeply entrenched destructive habits
    - inner wounding

34. Guilt is the easiest of these to remove, though it tends to receive the most attention. Guilt is removed by the truth and the cross.

35. I must first tell myself the truth about my sin. Then I can tell God the truth about it (repentance) and repent to those I have wronged.

36. Having told God the truth about my sin, in prayer I bring it to Christ on the cross. On the cross he made full provision for my guilt to be removed.

37. The process of removing my destructive habits is more extended. Jesus leads me into a life-long process of dying to the self-life, allowing the Holy Spirit to remake me.

38. Inner pain can block my maturing toward Christlikeness. Sin, mine and that of others around me, has wounded me. Healing comes in God's Presence.

39. Christlikeness is formed, not in the mind, but in a Relationship. I am with Jesus to learn from Jesus how to be like Jesus (Dallas Willard).

40. Discipleship to Jesus produces inwardly transformed people. I am inwardly transformed as I learn from Jesus how to live with him in God's Kingdom—in God's Presence.

CHAPTER ONE

Restore the Ancient Anointings

Elijah Was a Man with a Nature like Ours

1. I first heard the phrase "Restore the Ancient Anointings" while listening to a recorded message. The impact the words had on me initially has never subsided.

2. The phrase seemed to carry a prophetic call. It came during the early years of returning with Hanna to her home region of Germany—the Eifel.

3. To Hanna, a Jewish Holocaust survivor, the Eifel felt like a very dark place. She had lived her first seven years there under the Nazis.

4. In the year 2000 God began to lead her to return. We spent some days in her home town Gemünd. We had no idea what God was about to do.

5. We felt God leading us to return the following summer—2001. We began to pray at each place in Gemünd that held painful memories for Hanna.

6. Her family home had been on the Dreibornerstrasse. In the school yard Jewish children had been threatened. We prayed in the Jewish cemetery.

7. We went to the cinema where Hanna and her friend Ruth had been denied entrance to see *Snow White and the Seven Dwarfs*. No Jews allowed!

8. We prayed where the local synagogue had stood. Hanna used to walk there holding her father's hand. She was in Gemünd the night it was burned—"Crystal Night," November 9, 1938.

9. We invited Jesus into each space. We asked him to dispel the darkness, to come there with his redeeming Presence. Through prayer, healing went deeper.

10. I heard Hanna, a German-Jewish Holocaust survivor, begin to ask for God's blessing. "Come Lord Jesus. Heal the past, bless the people of the Eifel, manifest your kingdom."

11. A Jewish follower of the Jewish Messiah had returned, in fulfillment of God's calling to her people Israel—to bless the Gentiles (Gen. 12:3).

12. The next summer—2002—we felt the Lord leading us to return to Gemünd with intercessors. This was the beginning of five summers of prayer days in the Eifel.

13. In the year 2006 we sensed the Lord speaking through the words of Genesis 31:3, "Return to the land of your fathers...and I will be with you."

14. We asked the Lord what this meant. Where would we live? Where would the money come from? His answer: I will give you everything you need.

15. We rented an apartment in the village of Dahlem. We began to

spend 4-6 months a year in the Eifel in a ministry of forgiveness and reconciliation, praying for spiritual renewal.

16. What will it look like for God's blessing—his forgiveness, grace, healing, new life—to flow freely among the people of the Eifel?

17. Many will become alive in Christ. But that will present new challenges. Who among them will be able to disciple new believers to maturity?

18. The more we prayed the more we realized the Eifel was not yet ready for a new move of God. The next step was to make preparations—disciples.

When Christian Confession Does Not Mature Into Christlikeness

19. We had seen it all before. Great moves of God have turned into train-wrecks due to inadequately-formed character, especially among leaders.

20. In 1972, with Operation Mobilization, we went with the ship *Logos* to the Indonesian island of Timor. We had heard of a powerful move of the Spirit there—miracles, healings, etc.

21. Upon our arrival, we asked knowledgeable people about the revival. "It's over!" they said. Why? "Lust for power, sexual immorality, and greed."

22. Many years later we heard an Austrian historian speak on the causes of moral failure among Medieval clergy. Her conclusion: Lust for power, sexual immorality, greed.

23. Sadly this also describes well-known church situations in the US today. Leaders are being de-railed by lust for power, sexual immorality, greed.

24. How can this be? How can we study (and teach!) about Jesus, and still not get it? How can we act as though Christ-like character is irrelevant?

25. Can it be that multitudes never find their way to inner wholeness because they are being led and taught by ministers who have never found it themselves?

26. No. The Eifel was not yet ready for a move of God. This is a time for preparation. Ministers must be identified, discipled, and matured toward Christlikeness.

27. In this way, unknown to us, *Maturing toward Wholeness in the Inner Life* was in the process of being born.

Spiritual Strongholds—Hard Ground

28. Hanna and I spent the first 20 years of our ministry lives focused on evangelism. The beginning was in Europe—Italy, France, Belgium, UK, Eastern Europe, et. al.

29. Then Hanna spent two years in Israel. I went to India. Later she joined me there. We were married in the city of Hyderabad. We oversaw outreach teams throughout the country.

30. As senior leaders in Operation Mobilization, a ministry with some 2,000 workers, we also had in-depth relationships with others serving throughout the Middle East.

31. Europe. Middle East. India. Hard areas for evangelism. Little fruit. Why? Hard ground! The seed was being sown on soil that could benefit from more preparation.

32. One day in Bombay (today Mumbai) I organized local Christians to give out gospel tracts at city train stations. We gave out 500,000—in one day!

33. The next day I walked through the city. Was it any different? Had any of the seed taken root? I wonder the same today—almost 50 years later.

34. The next chapter in our lives was ships. In 1971 I was asked to be director of the Operation Mobilization ship *Logos*. Our ministry was evangelism and discipleship.

35. *Logos* carried 140 workers from 20 countries. We sought to focus on the hardest areas—Asia, India, Middle East, Europe.

36. God taught us how to develop leaders. We soon assembled the leadership core for a second ship. In 1977 God gave us *Doulos* with 325 workers.

37. We led the *Logos* and *Doulos* teams for fifteen years. The ships carried out 40 programs a year. We ministered in scores of countries.

38. In 1985 we completed our service with *Logos* and *Doulos*. God was taking us to his next assignment. In 1987 Antioch Network was born.

Ancient Anointings

39. Jesus preached the Gospel of the Kingdom. He used words, then demonstrated the kingdom's Presence through healings and other miracles.

40. Transformed lives manifest the kingdom's Presence. Christlikeness formed in broken people (all of us) is a miracle of healing.

41. Christlikeness is indispensable to:
    • the message preached
    • the preacher's life
    • the fruit of the preaching

- the Christian community

42. For years I held the historic church in dishonor. I saw her as being "dead!" I confess this to my shame. I repent, and ask God and brothers and sisters in historic churches for forgiveness.

43. God began to address my sin and ignorance by a trip through history. He began with the desert fathers. The life of St. Anthony gripped me.

44. Anthony of Egypt (251-356). The surrounding culture was forming Anthony apart from God. He chose not to allow it. He withdrew into the desert.

45. In the solitude of the desert God taught Anthony wisdom. Many sought him out. Some joined him. They became known as the desert fathers and mothers.

46. John the Beloved (6-100). Some view Anthony as heir to John's spiritual legacy. John leaned on Jesus' breast—the apostle of the contemplative life.

47. Polycarp (69-155) was John's spiritual son. John ordained him Bishop of Smyrna. Polycarp was burned at the stake for his faith at age 86.

48. Irenaeus (130-202), Bishop of Lyon, was discipled by Polycarp. So three generations after Jesus John's legacy had reached Anthony's century.

49. I sought to trace John's legacy beyond Anthony. Some historians suggest a close connection between the desert fathers and mothers and the Celtic Church.

50. Patrick of Ireland (389-461) was born in England. Sold into slavery in Ireland, he escaped, but later returned as a missionary bishop.

51. Patrick:
    - evangelized
    - founded churches
    - founded monasteries
    - did spiritual battle against paganism
    - became spiritual father to the Irish church

52. Patrick's apostolic authority was fueled by Trinitarian devotion. His *Breastplate* speaks powerfully of this. "I bind unto myself today the strong name of the Trinity."

53. Columba (521-597), one of the "Twelve Apostles of Ireland", founded a monastery at Iona in present-day Scotland. It became a center of Celtic worship and outreach.

54. Aidan (?-651), sent out from Iona, founded a monastery at Lindisfarne in northeast England. It too became a fountain of apostolic initiatives.

55. The spiritual vitality of the Celtic Church began to spill over into missionary initiatives to northern England and the continent of Europe.

56. Willibrord (658-739) evangelized in the Eifel! In the village of Daufenbach he planted a cross at a pagan worship site in a river and baptized converts.

57. I share all this only to chronicle a journey toward understanding through which God was taking me. One more short dip into Church history before we leave.

58. We Protestants have inherited a narrative that the Catholic Church of Luther's day (1483-1546) was characterized only by spiritual deadness.

59. The Bible came to Luther through the Catholic Church. Catholic reformers preceded him such as John Wycliff (1320-1384) and Jan

Hus (1369-1415).

60. Teresa of Avila (1515-1582) was Catholic. Protestant scholar Dallas Willard said he learned more about the soul from her than from anyone else.

61. Ignatius Loyola (1491-1556) was Catholic. His insights into spiritual formation have been widely embraced across the Christian traditions.

62. John of the Cross (1542-1591) was Catholic. His work *Dark Night of the Soul* is considered a classic by Protestants and Catholics alike.

63. Abraham, Moses, Ruth, David, Elijah, Mary, John, Polycarp, Anthony, Patrick, Martin Luther, Teresa of Avila, John Wesley, Amy Carmichael, Martin Luther King, Billy Graham.

64. God's anointing—his hand upon individuals—permeates 4,000 years of Judeo-Christian history, reaching across the Christian traditions.

Revisiting "Hard Ground": The Ministry of Reconciliation

65. Hanna and I began with evangelism. We learned about hard ground. Much later, we began to understand how reconciliation affects evangelism. It can prepare the ground.

66. Jesus preached the Gospel of the Kingdom. Then he demonstrated the kingdom's presence. Reconciliation demonstrates the kingdom's presence.

67. Rebelling against our Creator has left mankind tragically fragmented. Relational hostility permeates families, societies, nations, churches.

68. Violent acts and vengeful responses solidify hatreds and harden the ground for the Gospel. Christ's cross has the power to break spiritual strongholds and transform them.

69. Reconciliation is needed everywhere—in marriage and family, with those whom we or our ancestors have wronged, in our society, among the nations.

70. Our greatest need is to be reconciled to God. We violated him by our arrogance, rebellion and folly. Oneness with him was severed—the choice that so damaged us.

71. God has initiated reconciliation. We are the ones who went away from him. He is the One who came seeking a restored relationship with us. In Jesus he carried the effects of our sin.

72. Now he waits. Whether to accept his offer of reconciliation is our decision. He doesn't pressure. Reconciliation must be freely chosen.

73. By experiencing our relationship with God being restored, we learn how to proceed in being reconciled with others. Jesus teaches us how.

74. Hanna's parents were gassed in the death camp at Chelmno, Poland, on May 3, 1942. On May 3, 2015 she read from her book in the city of Bonn, Germany, in a public meeting.

75. When she finished, Markus, a German businessman, approached the microphone. "Hanna, my grandfather was an SS Officer at Chelmno when your parents were there."

76. Markus: "I don't know what to say. I can only stand here and say the words my grandfather never said. Will you forgive me?" Hanna rose and went to him. "I forgive you." They embraced.

77. With tears the grandson of a German SS Officer asked forgiveness of a Jewish Holocaust survivor. She forgave him. The ground became softer.

78. Over the last 500 years the number of Christian denominations has been multiplying. Too often divisions are deep and bitter. We have said and done terrible things to each other.

79. The world watches. Hostility between Christians denies the Gospel. In many cases it has entrenched historic roots formed by what we have said and done—spiritual strongholds.

80. As hate-filled battles between Christians dissolve into repentance, forgiveness, mutual honoring and love, the ground will soften noticeably!

81. Jesus: "I in them and you in me, that they may become perfectly one, so that the world may know that you sent me" (Jn. 17:23a).

82. Reconciliation is an expression of Christ-like character. We learn it in discipleship with Jesus. He becomes our Master Teacher in how to live.

Discipleship — Christ-like Character Formed in the Inner Life

83. How important is Christlikeness formed in the inner life? #1. It is what discipleship to Jesus is all about—its purpose and end result.

84. How important is Christlikeness formed in the inner life? #2. It alone can bring meaning, healing, purpose and joy to the individual.

85. How important is Christlikeness formed in the inner life? #3. As the Gospel is preached it manifests the Presence and power of the kingdom.

86. How important is Christlikeness formed in the inner life? #4. It provides the Church with the leaders she needs to bring her to maturity.

87. How important is Christlikeness formed in the inner life? #5. Without it any new move of the Spirit is in great danger of ending badly.

88. Jesus: "A disciple is not above his teacher, but everyone when he is fully trained will be like his teacher" (Lk. 6:40).

CHAPTER TWO

Discipleship

Becoming Able to Live the Way Jesus Said Was Best

1. Wholeness in the inner life is Christlikeness in the inner life. It develops as we learn to allow Jesus to teach us how to live.

2. God did not give commandments because he enjoys making us do things we don't want to do. They inform us how human life is designed to work.

3. Jesus: "A new commandment I give to you, that you love one another" (Jn. 13:34). Anger, hatred, envy, contempt—these don't fulfill us. Love does!

4. Jesus and the apostles spoke of a life lived in personal relationship with God, characterized by fulfillment, joy, meaning, and wholeness.

5. The life Jesus offers us is one lived each moment in God's Presence. There he teaches us how to actually do what he said was best.

6. As we allow Jesus to teach us how to do life, moral victory (not perfection) develops. We learn how to respond well to whatever life brings.

7. Many seem to feel wholeness in life is unattainable. Even ones who self-identify as Christians often abandon hope of personal victory. Why?

8. Having been created by God to be like him and to live in his Presence, each of us made the disastrous decision to go away from him.

9. We pushed back from God and sought a life of our own making. We went our own way. We thought we knew better how to find pleasure—happiness.

10. My choice to break with God resulted not only in guilt, but also in extensive damage to my thoughts, emotions, will, body, and relationships.

11. My inner life has been deeply shaped by a world of wrongness— dysfunction both within me and in those around me. It now must be re-formed.

12. Re-forming the inner life is an indispensable component of the biblical processes of salvation and sanctification. It takes place in apprenticeship to Jesus.

13. Jesus came to restore to us the life God originally created us to have. This is salvation in its fullest sense. It involves four processes.

14. New life from God grows in me as:
    • guilt is removed
    • impurity is cleansed
    • inner wounds are healed
    • each part of my being is re-made

15. Parts of me needing to be re-made:
    • heart (will)
    • soul
    • mind (thoughts, emotions)
    • strength (body)
    • relationships (neighbor)

16. Jesus outlined the parts/components of a human person in responding to the scribe who asked which commandment was most important (Mk. 12:28-31).

17. As healing, and then newness of life, invade my heart, soul, mind, body and relationships, I become able from the heart to love God and my neighbor.

18. These all point in different ways to the same reality:
    • salvation (deliverance) in its fullest sense
    • re-formation
    • transformation
    • restoration

19. In the Bible salvation means deliverance. Delivered from what? Guilt? Yes! Is that all? No! Also from bondage to the practice of sin (Rom. 6:6).

20. Israel's salvation mirrors the Christian life. God:
    • delivered them from slavery
    • formed them in the desert
    • gave them the good land

21. Christ:
    • by his cross saves us from all sin's effects
    • in discipleship trains us how to access this gift
    • by grace gives us a new life

22. This all comes to us by grace. We can never earn it, but we must choose it. Faith is a daily condition we choose to walk in, expressed

by our actions.

23. God is a gentleman. He does not force his will on us. He respects our decisions. He offers us newness of life—then awaits our response.

24. Being remade into Christlikeness is a lifelong process. It has a beginning. It may have spiritual highs. But they cannot bypass the process.

25. I am remade into a new person as I allow Jesus to teach me how to live. He is the wisest Teacher in all of history—no one else comes close.

26. I gradually learn to rely on Jesus. His cross removes my guilt. His Presence cleanses me. His teachings instruct me. His Spirit re-forms me.

27. My will must be fully engaged. I must choose God's way each moment. The Holy Spirit will not do this "to" me or "for" me—only "with" me.

28. I must distinguish "will" (choice) from "will-power" (trying harder). Willpower cannot change me. It is self-reliance. It leads only to frustration and defeat.

29. I cannot, on the spur of the moment, decide by willpower to run a marathon. But I can choose to train, and in time become the kind of person who is able to run one.

30. The Christian life is about the person I am becoming. I must choose it, but I don't do it. The Holy Spirit does it in apprenticeship to Jesus.

CHAPTER THREE

Humility

Living in Harmony with What Is True About God and Me

1. Humility is neither mysterious nor unattainable. As I mature toward Christlikeness, it increasingly characterizes the person I am becoming.

2. Humility is central to who Jesus is. Being found in human form, he humbled himself (Php. 2:8). Growth in Christlikeness is growth in humility.

3. Isaiah had a profound experience of God. It gave him deeper insight into God and himself. It left him with a new depth in humility (Isa. 6:1-5).

4. Job had a similar experience to Isaiah (Job 42:5-6). So did Paul (2 Cor. 12:1-10). So do all who deeply experience the Presence of God.

5. Humility is simply living in sync with what is true—about God and about me. It is the condition God designed me to have when he created me.

6. The two opposites to humility—1) pride (self-worship) and 2) inferiority (self-hatred)—can only exist when I am out of touch with reality.

7. What is true of God and me? First, I am a created being. I am not God; I am not self-determined; I am not self-sufficient.

8. I can make my own decisions because God gave me this ability. But I do not control the consequences that result from my decisions. God does.

9. I am a glorious being, created by an indescribably magnificent God in his own likeness. He designed me to live continually in his Presence.

10. God trusted me, with my fellow human beings, to have dominion over his creation, the work of his hands. What high esteem he has for me/us!

11. I am like every other human. I have no ability I was not given. I have no basis for pride. In relation to others I am *unique* not *better*.

12. I am a fallen glorious being. I chose to go away from my heavenly Father, to leave his Presence, to try to make a better life for myself.

13. My first parents, Adam and Eve, also chose to go away from God. But blaming others will not help me. It was my choice; I alone am responsible.

14. My choice to leave my Father's Presence was insane! What was I thinking? That I knew better? It led to such damage in me and others near me.

15. I am unable to reverse the effects of my wrong choices by myself. Wounding within keeps me from finding my way back home to God's Presence. I am lost.

16. Mankind's understanding is shattered in two crucial areas as we are disconnected from:
    - the height of our glory
    - the depth of our ruin

17. My heavenly Father has made a Way for me to return home and live again in his Presence—a gift of utter mercy and grace. This Way is Jesus.

18. In Jesus:
    - my guilt can be removed
    - my impurities can be cleansed
    - my wounds can be healed
    - power of sin in my behavior can be broken
    - my bad choices can be redeemed
    - my Father's likeness can be re-formed in me

19. We seem easily to become aware of our brokenness, even in the midst of heavy denial. It is much harder to connect with our God-given worth.

20. Do I really have value? Am I worthy of being loved? I so desperately need to hear "I love you" and know it was my Father who said it.

21. Hearing my Creator say "I love you" happens as I practice his Presence. There I experience the love, value, delight he feels toward me.

22. Unable to connect with my innate and indestructible value, I will lapse into arrogance or self-hatred. My need to be treasured is that great.

23. Striving to meet my own need for self-worth, I tend to search for significance by what I can achieve. This often leads to addiction to *doing*.

24. I may look to others—even try to manipulate them into expressing

value for me. This can trap me in harmful behavior and relationships.

25. Humility is a condition of my being, not of my behavior. Trying to *act* humble only leads to false humility, easily recognized by others.

26. Humility is a condition of the soul. Mary: My soul magnifies the Lord...for he has looked on the humble estate of his servant (Lk. 1:46).

27. A person maturing toward humility is largely unaware of it. There may be moments of insight, but it will be clear that whatever humility is in me is a work of God's grace.

28. As we grow in humility, our thoughts are less and less of ourselves and more and more of God and others. This is the cure for narcissism!

29. Humility is cultivated in solitude. Withdrawing from other voices enables me to hear better the Voice that speaks Truth to me—that heals me.

30. Humility is cultivated in worship. Connecting with God, I become aware of:
   • how great he is
   • how finite I am
   • how highly he esteems me

CHAPTER FOUR

The Kingdom of God

Unseen Reality

1. Jesus began his ministry the same way John the Baptist did. He announced that the kingdom of God was at hand—accessible like never before.

2. Jesus used kingdom "of God" and "of heaven" interchangeably. (Mt. 4:17; Mk. 1:15) The kingdom was at hand because the King was at hand.

3. We had turned from God's rule and gone our own way. Now Jesus was inviting us to turn again—Repent!—and enter through him into the kingdom.

4. The kingdom of God, or heaven, is the foundational theme integrating all Jesus' teaching. The terms are found over 80 times in the Gospels.

5. Major portions of Jesus' teaching describe God's kingdom, in-

cluding the Sermon on the Mount, perhaps the most influential talk in all of human history.

6. "Blessed are those who mourn" (Mt. 5:4). Was Jesus saying, "Go and mourn?" Or did he mean, "Those who are mourning have the option of receiving comfort in God's kingdom?"

7. God's kingdom is the sphere in which God's rule is unopposed—where what God wants to happen happens without resistance or rebellion.

8. There is another kingdom, in rebellion against God's rule—a kingdom of spiritual darkness and limited power. God allows this for a time.

9. To resist the kingdom of darkness in our own strength is presumptuous—dangerous. We come against it by invoking the power of Christ's cross.

10. God gave mankind dominion over (responsibility for) creation. We opened ourselves to the ruler of the darkness. Now the world lies in the grip of evil (Rom. 8:20).

11. Christ came to destroy the devil's work, save us from bondage to evil, and restore us to our original state—eternal life in God's kingdom.

12. God's kingdom is eternal. Like God himself, it has always been and always will be. It existed before the material world and will outlast it.

13. God's kingdom is real. We sometimes say we must live in the *real world*. God's kingdom is the *real world*—it is the ultimate reality.

14. God's kingdom is unseen. This should not surprise us. God is unseen. He created the material world but he is not part of it. God

is Spirit.

15. Though God's kingdom is unseen, activity there produces visible, tangible results. Jesus said in order to meet material needs, rely on the kingdom! (Mt. 6:25-34)

16. Jesus:
    • called us to repentance
    • announced the kingdom's availability
    • revealed the kingdom's presence by healing and casting out demons

17. We are not only to proclaim the kingdom (word) but also reveal the kingdom (act). Lives re-formed in Christlikeness reveal the kingdom.

18. The worldview today that dismisses Unseen Reality has ushered us into a great unreality. In our pride of life we grope in darkness.

19. Jesus prayed. Spiritual fathers and mothers throughout Judeo-Christian millennia have prayed. Asking, relying on God, we access the kingdom.

20. God's kingdom is filled with his Presence. To accept God's rule is to live in his Presence. To resist his rule is to turn from his Presence.

21. Adam and Eve, listening to the voice from the darkness, decided in favor of self-rule. This choice separated them from God's Presence.

22. Jesus came:
    • to be the Way for mankind to re-enter God's kingdom
    • to teach us how to live there once we arrive
    He is the Door in.

23. Self-rule renders us unable to live in sync with the ways of God's kingdom. By the time we realize this, self-rule is rooted deeply within.

24. Self-rule and self-reliance are two sides of the same coin. Relying on God may feel scary at first. Relying on self is what is truly scary.

25. In his opening public statement Jesus gave the key to kingdom entry: "Repent!" (Mt. 4:17). Repent of what? Of self-rule and self-reliance!

26. God's rule is full of kindness, wisdom, goodness. He created us free to choose. He does not force his rule on us. He awaits our response.

27. We are free to choose but we are not free to avoid the consequences of our choices. Jesus warned about the unintended consequences of self-rule.

28. God's kingdom is shaped by God's character. The ways of the kingdom are ways of holiness (absence of impurity) and love (absence of self).

29. Jesus likened the kingdom of heaven to treasure hidden in a field. A man found it, sold all he had and bought the field (Mt. 13:44). Smart man!

30. Entering into and living in God's kingdom will cost us our old life. This enables us to receive a new life—God's eternal life (Mt. 16:24-25).

31. Jesus went to all the cities and villages:
    • teaching
    • proclaiming the gospel of the kingdom
    • healing every affliction (Mt. 9:35)

CHAPTER FIVE

Practicing God's Presence

Where I Am Re-Formed

1. I have been created to be like God, and to live continually in his Presence. These two reinforce each other.

2. The more time I spend in God's Presence, the more I become like him. The more I become like him, the more I desire to be in his Presence.

3. Why then does entering God's Presence and staying there seem so hard, so unnatural? Because I chose to go away from him. This damaged me.

4. Separated from God's Presence, our inner lives became badly distorted. Trying to find our way on our own, harmful habits took root within.

5. Distanced from Reality, being with God came to seem undesirable—unobtainable. Our need now is to be forgiven, cleansed, healed, re-formed.

6. David's capacity to sin showed the state of his inner life. "Create in me a clean heart, O God, and renew a right spirit within me" (Ps. 51:10).

7. Learning how to live in God's Presence involves daily:
   • dying with Christ to the old life
   • relying on Christ for his resurrection life

8. Isn't God everywhere? Surely I am always in his Presence. In one sense this is true. But we are referring to "presence" in another sense.

9. Two people can be in the same room yet one not be *present* to the other. One can be relationally withdrawn while still physically *there*.

10. Humans can go away from God's Presence. "Cain went away from the presence of the Lord and settled in the land of Nod" (Gen. 4:6).

11. God is always and everywhere present to us, but we are not always present to him. In our ruined state we have learned to "block him out."

12. Practicing God's Presence involves choosing actions to:
    • un-learn blocking God out
    • re-learn coming present to him and staying there

13. God is Spirit. He does not normally make himself present to us through our physical senses, although he certainly can whenever he wishes.

14. To practice God's Presence:
    • I rely on the fact that God is there
    • I choose actions to help place my thoughts on him and keep them there

15. As my thoughts wander from God, I learn to train them to return in shorter and shorter intervals. I ask the Spirit to transform my thoughts.

16. In what way is all this "practice"? Learning any skill is practice: playing an instrument, speaking a language, mastering a sport, becoming a surgeon.

17. To un-learn the wrong, then re-learn the right, some instruction is required. But there is no substitute for practice, practice, practice.

18. Practice—moment by moment choices to establish new habits—is key to inner change. The Holy Spirit does the work; my choices invite him in.

19. The Bible tells us to pray without ceasing (1 Thess. 5:17), abide in Christ (Jn. 15:4), be filled with the Spirit (Eph. 5:18). Each requires being in God's Presence.

20. These are all commands—activities for which we are responsible, relying on God. They describe "practicing" or "living in" God's Presence.

21. Prerequisite for living in God's Presence is knowing how to access his forgiveness and cleansing. The cross of Christ accomplishes this.

22. In prayer I bring sins of which I am aware to Christ on the cross. I tell him the truth (confession). I ask for forgiveness and cleansing. I trust him to hear and respond.

23. Having brought my sin to Christ on the cross, I thank him for his forgiveness. I then wait to hear anything more he would say to me. I obey.

24. As I bring my sins to Christ on the cross, I may not feel anything. Feelings are not required; truth in the inner life is required.

25. The healing of my person begins when:
    • I come into God's Presence
    • I listen for the healing word he is always ready to speak
    • I obey

26. I cannot heal myself. I cannot make myself holy. But I can learn how to obey. Jesus teaches me how in apprenticeship to him.

27. Practicing God's Presence is supported by spiritual exercises—activities for training the inner life—disciplines we learn from Jesus.

28. Spiritual practices—prayer, study, fasting, giving, etc.—have no power to earn me favor with God. Nothing does! Favor with God is a gift.

29. We freely choose spiritual practices:
    • to counteract the effects of inner damage
    • to open our lives to God's transforming Presence

30. Exercises for training the spirit are similar to exercises for training the body. Dallas Willard: "Grace is not opposed to effort; grace is opposed to earning."

31. "You make known to me the path of life; in your presence there is fullness of joy; at your right hand are pleasures forevermore" (Ps. 16:11).

CHAPTER SIX

Faith

Choosing to Rely on God for Forgiveness of Sin and Everything Else

1. God created our first parents for a life filled with delight, meaning, joy and love. They were to receive this life by continually relying on him.

2. But Adam and Eve decided to turn from God and go their own way. They thought they knew better. They chose to rely on themselves.

3. This was a disastrous decision! It left them guilty before God. But it did more. Cut off from God's wisdom, they kept making bad choices. We have all done the same.

4. Self-reliance became deeply embedded in humanity, resulting in further dysfunction. We make our own decisions—and they damage us.

5. Self-reliance is an expression of self-will. Self-will is an expression of self-worship, our core idolatry, the evil that has distorted us.

6. Jesus called his hearers to repent and rely on God's rule. Repent of what? Of what prevents us from receiving from God; self-worship. Discipleship is lived in a posture of repentance.

7. Self-reliance surfaces early. Toddlers are often very self-assertive. They need to be protected from the harm self-reliance ultimately causes.

8. God in Christ is redeeming humanity. On the cross Jesus' made provision for:
   • our sins to be forgiven
   • God's life to be re-formed in us

9. The offer of this redemption is a Father's gift. We can't earn it. We can only say "yes" to it. We gain access to it by faith.

10. What is faith? Mental ascent? Yes, but more than that. It is belief that leads to relying on what is believed. Faith without works is dead (Jm. 2:17).

11. I can "believe" China has over 1 billion people. If census workers made a mistake I don't lose anything. I am not invested in this belief.

12. I can "believe" that a rope bridge over a canyon can support me. If I choose to walk across the bridge I am relying on what I believe.

13. Faith is choosing to rely on God–in everything! It is a moment by moment default setting we learn from Jesus. He taught it. He lived it.

14. Faith is God-reliance:
    • for my sins to be forgiven
    • for my bondage to sinful behavior to be broken
    • It is a heart transaction that cannot choose one but reject the other.

15. Wanting to "believe" in Christ for eternal life, but holding on to sinful behavior, is not what God is offering. This is just another form of self-will.

16. I cannot rely on God and disobey him. Why would I disobey God? Because I think my way, not his way, is best for me. This is simply relying on self.

17. Biblical faith is expressed by obedience. Obedience is an outflow of biblical faith. If I trust God I will want to live the way he says is best.

18. Christ takes away our sin. How?
    • He takes away our guilt.
    • He takes away our sinful behavior.
    • Relying on him we come to share his life.

19. So many "believers" are in bondage to sinful behavior. Why? We have by-passed discipleship. In discipleship we learn from Jesus how the power of sin in our behavior is broken.

20. In the life of faith we choose to rely on God apart from what our five senses seem to be telling us. We walk by faith, not by sight (2 Cor. 5:7).

21. God is Spirit. He is not part of the physical world, though he created the physical world, is everywhere present in the physical world, and reveals himself in the physical world as he wills.

22. The idea that the only reality is physical reality cannot be proven and is simply untrue. Christ is risen and is everywhere present (Mt. 28:20).

23. "Proof" of the Unseen Real is transformed lives throughout the centuries. The facts are in the public record for any who will examine them.

24. Living by self-reliance results in personal crisis when faced with serious accident, illness, job loss, family tensions, old age, etc.

25. What ever made me think that relying on myself was a good idea? Far more "logical" is to rely on God who created me, is all-powerful, and is always with me.

26. Some view faith as a one-time act. This is how many understand it. Many others cannot identify a time when they "first believed."

27. However it begins, faith must mature–from being one act, to occurring in fits and starts, to becoming our habitual response to every occasion.

28. We meet Christ by relying on him. We live with Christ by relying on him. "As you received Christ Jesus the Lord, so walk in him" (Col. 2:6).

29. Learning how to rely on God is closely related to learning how to live in his Presence. Jesus teaches us how in discipleship to him.

30. Faith is not established primarily through analytical thinking, although this is involved. Faith is established by being with God—by being in the Presence.

31. In the Presence we experience God. This forms us more deeply than analysis ever could. We know we have been with God and that we can trust him.

32. We discover the Bible is God's word when we meet God there. We come to know on a level that does not violate our reason–but is deeper.

33. Unbelief is not essentially a mental problem but a moral problem–a sin problem. One determined to sin—to live in self-will—will distance himself from faith.

34. Learning how to rely on God is closely related to learning how to live with him in his kingdom. Jesus teaches us how in discipleship to him.

35. Learning how to rely on God is closely related to learning how to pray without ceasing. Jesus teaches us how in discipleship to him.

36. A life lived relying on God is filled with peace, sanity, order and blessing. Jesus promised us, "Peace I leave with you; my peace I give to you" (Jn. 14:27).

37. A life lived in self-will creates disorder, alienation, unresolved pain. News headlines almost daily report prominent people badly malfunctioning.

38. Jesus lived relying on his Father. "The Son can do nothing of his own accord, but only what he sees the Father doing" (Jn. 5:19). He calls us to do likewise. "Apart from me you can do nothing" (Jn. 15:5).

CHAPTER SEVEN

Inner Healing

Healing the Pain That Is Blocking My Maturity

1. At some point, living as Christ's disciple, I am likely to become aware of wounded areas within that are hindering or blocking my maturing.

2. Craziness began when I turned from God and went my own way. Sanity is gradually being restored as I learn how to rely on Jesus to teach me how life works.

3. My destructive behaviors are rooted in:
   • my own sin
   • sin done against me
   • my sinful responses to sin done against me
   • sin all around me in family and society

4. I am wounded by inability to accept myself. I am out of touch with the person I truly am, created in the likeness of a magnificent God.

5. I am wounded by expecting or demanding that other people meet

my needs. I am looking to the wrong person. Only God can meet my needs.

6. I am wounded by self-centeredness (introspection, narcissism). I am looking at the wrong person. Jesus leads me into a God-centered life.

7. I am wounded by dishonoring my parents. If I am unable to relate well with them, I will tend to relate in unhealthy ways with other authorities. This can further damage me (see Chapter 22).

8. I am wounded by anger, contempt and bitterness. These are violent behaviors; they trigger violence in return. People don't enjoy being around an angry person.

9. I am wounded by sexual violation—what I may have committed or what I may have suffered. God created sexuality to express a unique intimacy (see Chapter 19).

10. I am wounded by shame. Shame keeps me from being honest about my need and seeking help. It expresses a distorted understanding of myself.

11. I am wounded by inability to forgive—to commit my enemy to God and leave payback to him. God is Judge—a role he has not assigned to me (see Chapter 20).

12. I am wounded by inability to receive forgiveness. I cannot deserve forgiveness; it is a gift God, and others, offer me. I just need to gratefully receive it. I may need to forgive myself.

13. I am wounded by assuming a victim role. If I am a child of God I am never a victim. Why? I have a Heavenly Father—all-powerful, all-knowing, all-compassionate. I choose to trust him.

14. My Heavenly Father has allowed what happened to me for reasons

only he fully understands. I may gain more insight as time goes by—or maybe never.

15. Could it be that my own behavior and responses played a role in the wrong done? What is the objective truth? Do I see all this accurately?

16. God is good, always with me, always protecting me, working all things for my good. To respond correctly to what I can't understand is crucial for my healing (Ps. 23:6).

17. Unhealed places within trap me in immature thinking and reacting. Unresolved childhood pain easily erupts in childish adult behavior—the experience of the adult child.

18. Unhealed places within me energize addictions—deeply entrenched habits I use to block out or escape pain. I soon find myself in bondage to them.

19. Unhealed places within me lead to wounding other people. When anger lies near the surface, it is easily triggered. Wounded people wound people.

20. Unhealed places within me hinder ministry. I lack insight as to why I, and others, behave as we do. I have a log in my eye (Mt. 7:1-5). Self-control eludes me.

21. I am healed by coming present to God and remaining there (see Chapter 5). I hear my Father say "I love you." I come to believe him. Healing goes deeper.

22. I am healed by listening for words of healing insight my Father is always ready to speak. I hear loving, specific correction. I obey.

23. I am healed by bringing my sins to Jesus on the cross. Guilt and habitual sin block healing and wound anew. The cross has broken sin's power.

24. I am healed by bringing my past wounding to Jesus on the cross. I bring him the painful memories. I ask him to step into them with me and heal them.

25. I am healed by forgiving those who have wronged me. I do not deny or minimize the wrong. I own what is true. But I leave "pay back"—judgment—to God.

26. I am healed by living daily as Jesus' apprentice. He teaches me how to avoid harmful behaviors and follow ways that lead to wholeness.

27. Jesus is the most skilled therapist in all of history. His teachings show:
    • how we are made
    • what went wrong
    • how we can be healed, redeemed, transformed

28. As I mature in the life of God, I come to see that I have been wounded more by my own wrong responses than by the actions of others.

29. I have no control over the actions of others. They are not my responsibility. My well-being cannot depend on what is not my responsibility—the actions and choices of others.

30. My well-being depends on my own actions and choices. Someone else chooses to harm me. Now it is my turn to choose how I am going to respond. Jesus teaches me how.

31. We are not healed by analytical thinking—even analyzing the Bible. Living in our heads is not enough. We are healed by living in the Presence.

32. We are not healed by counseling, though godly counsellors can be a great help. We are healed by living in the Presence.

33. Jesus:
- announced the gospel of the kingdom
- taught the characteristics of the kingdom
- revealed the presence of the kingdom by healing (Mt. 9:35-36)

CHAPTER EIGHT

Spiritual Practices

Exercises for Inviting God's Healing Presence into My Inner Life

1. Spiritual practices are exercises to facilitate spiritual growth. We learn them from Jesus and our Judeo-Christian fathers and mothers.

2. Spiritual practices have been used for millennia—Abraham on a pilgrimage; Moses in the desert; David in the pasture; Jesus in the garden.

3. Spiritual practices serve to
   • counteract the effects of our fallenness
   • open our lives to the healing, transforming Presence of God.

4. Spiritual practices must be chosen voluntarily. They cannot be forced on me. What is forced on me by-passes my will—it is not really *me*.

5. The healing and transformation of my person must be directed by my will—my choices. Re-forming my person begins with the re-

forming of my will.

6. Spiritual practices have no power at all to help me gain favor with God. They are like the exercises an athlete uses to train his or her body.

7. We must avoid legalism at all costs—believing that doing a certain thing will make us more righteous before God. This is only self-reliance.

8. I can do nothing to make myself more righteous before God except to rely continually on him as he transforms me. Jesus teaches me how.

9. Spiritual practices have also been called "spiritual disciplines." One protection against legalism—allow love to supersede the discipline.

10. In love Jesus set aside the practice of Sabbath in order to heal. He interrupted times of solitude to respond to the needs of the crowds.

11. Time-proven ways to open my inner life to God prevent him from only being an abstraction. He is calling me into a relationship of intimacy.

12. It is tragic when God is only a concept, a theological proposition, a part of my upbringing, but I do not experience living in his Presence.

13. When ways to invite God into my inner life are not being practiced, the dysfunctions that have negatively shaped me remain unaddressed.

14. Resource books on spiritual practices: *Celebration of Discipline* by Richard Foster and *The Spirit of the Disciplines* by Dallas Willard.

15. There is no complete list of these practices, but it is helpful to group them into disciplines of abstinence and engagement.

16. Disciplines of abstinence are practices to weaken or break the power of habits that hinder or block my ability to live in God's Presence.

17. Practices of abstinence are for emptying. Solitude, fasting, chastity are some examples. The Spirit removes the old and Christ's death works in me.

18. Disciplines of engagement are practices to open my inner life more fully to God's Presence and support me as I learn how to live there 24/7.

19. Practices of engagement are for filling. Study, celebration, and prayer are some examples. The Spirit imparts the new and Christ's life works in me.

20. What I do with my body affects my soul. Using my body to sin, I wound my soul. Using my body to place myself in God's Presence leads to healing within my soul.

21. The parts of my person involved in spiritual practices:
    • will—I choose to seek God
    • body—I act on my choice with my body
    • soul—I welcome God into my person

22. Solitude (abstinence)—I withdraw for a time from social contact, physical movement, and sounds, except perhaps the gentle sounds of nature.

23. Solitude—Being still and quiet before God, I allow my soul to come to rest and clarity. I ask the Holy Spirit for healing insight and I obey.

24. Solitude—In a way solitude is an entry point into other practices. A life organized around listening to God will yield a heart of wisdom.

25. Fasting (abstinence)—I refuse food for a time. This reinforces my ability to focus on God. I use each bodily impulse for food to turn my thoughts to him.

26. Fasting—I learn that I am not bound by the demands of my body. I do not have contempt for my body, but I discover its appropriate place in God.

27. Fasting—Like other practices, fasting should begin in moderation and develop naturally. We can fast from things other than food—for example media, etc.

28. Study (engagement)—I work to reshape my thinking. Old thought patterns rooted in unreality are harmful. I work to establish new ways of thinking. I prioritize the Bible.

29. Study—I seek more than knowledge. When I don't understand something I don't rely only on my analytical mind. I ask the Spirit for insight.

30. Study—I am discerning about Christian books. I gravitate toward classics of proven value over time. In new books I look for old wisdom.

31. Study—Modern "wisdom" says read as many books as possible. The result can be much superficiality. It might be better to focus on proven texts and go deep.

32. Study—I seek to go below the surface and enter into the author's thought patterns. I ask "Where did he or she get that?" I ask God for wisdom.

33. Celebration (engagement)—There is value in the parallel practice of abstinence and engagement. Celebration is a counterbalance to fasting.

34. Celebration—If I am unable to celebrate, I may not yet be ready

41

to fast. The wisdom of the centuries is found in the church year which includes both feasts and fasts.

35. Celebration—Teresa of Avila expressed joy in both fasting and celebrating. She said, "When I fast, I fast; and when I eat partridge, I eat partridge."

36. Focus and intensity, not compulsivity and heroics, are key in spiritual practices. I can't have a shower that does me any good if I only get one drop of water a minute.

CHAPTER NINE

Solitude

Ushering My Soul into the Healing Silences of God

1. I can expect at some point in life to long to go deeper with God. But I will need help in how to proceed. Solitude offers a time-tested way.

2. What I have experienced in life with God up to now may have left me empty and unfulfilled. There may be unwanted behaviors I am unable to change.

3. In solitude I withdraw, for a time, from social contact, physical movement, and sounds (except perhaps from the gentle sounds of nature).

4. I offer my time and myself to God as a gift of love. Waiting in quietness and stillness, my soul comes to rest. It then reaches new clarity.

5. For millennia solitude and silence have shaped the lives of our fathers and mothers in the Judeo-Christian faith. Silence com-

pletes solitude.

6. Moses—God took him from Pharaoh's court and formed him 40 years in the desert. God was shaping one of history's most influential leaders.

7. Being still before God can feel like a waste of time—we have so much to do! Compulsivity to achieve is driven by an unmet need to be loved.

8. Judeo-Christian history shows that ones who have been with God, although not motivated by achievement, have led amazingly influential lives.

9. David—His "desert" was pasturelands tending sheep. In stillness God imparted to him the foundations of Judeo-Christian worship—the Psalms.

10. Elijah—Formed in hiddenness, God entrusted to him unusual spiritual authority. Elijah was used to turn Israel from entrenched apostasy.

11. John the Baptist—In the wilderness until his public appearance, he catalyzed a powerful movement. His only resource—God's hand upon him.

12. Jesus—Like John, Jesus spent his formative years away from the limelight. Preparing to be tested by Satan, he withdrew into the desert.

13. Jesus regularly retreated into solitude, emerged for ministry, then withdrew again. Before choosing the twelve he spent the night in prayer (see Mk. 1:35-39, 6:30-34; Lk. 6:12-13).

14. To prepare for his greatest trial, Jesus withdrew to the stillness of the garden. He knew his greatest need was to be with his Father.

15. Paul—Confronted by Christ on the road to Damascus, he had much healing and re-forming to work through. God led him into the Arabian desert.

16. Later in life, forced by imprisonment to set aside his intense activity, Paul accomplished his most fruitful and enduring work—his writings.

17. Anthony of Egypt—In the 3rd and 4th centuries believers faced a violent, hedonistic Roman culture. Anthony determined not to allow it to form him.

18. Anthony and friends withdrew in solitude to the deserts of Egypt, Syria and Palestine, seeking intimacy with God and knowledge of his ways.

19. Crowds went out seeking wisdom from Anthony and the Desert Fathers and Mothers. Monasticism, one of history's most transformative movements, was born.

20. Anthony and his companions were heirs to the apostolic legacy of John the Beloved. "He who leans on Jesus' breast hears the heart of God."

21. Solitude and silence distance me from the activity and noise all around. Busyness, without counterbalancing stillness before God, wars against the soul.

22. Solitude and silence usher me into the healing silences of God. I am positioned to hear my Father say "I love you"—so foundational for my healing.

23. My compulsivity is energized by attempts to gain the love I desperately need. Others cannot meet this need—it is too great. God can!

24. Solitude and silence offer my body the rest it needs. This increases

my ability to be with God and hear him. Here is the principle of Sabbath.

25. Much illness is due to the stress compulsive "doing" inflicts on our bodies. When the soul is disordered, the body is used in unhealthy ways.

26. God worked for six days; then he rested. He told us to do the same. We are created to be like him. There is a rest for the people of God.

27. What does it say about Christian faith today that one of our greatest dangers is burnout? To whom are we listening? Whom are we following?

28. Solitude and silence make space for the kind of meditation that leads to wisdom. I live from my depths, much of which I don't yet understand.

29. Solitude and silence create space for listening for what God wants to say to me. One difficulty in hearing God—busyness keeps me distracted.

30. Solitude and silence are especially important for ones called to prophetic roles. It is crucial not only to hear God, but to hear him correctly.

31. Caution: We are not speaking here of introspection. In introspection my focus is on me. This only leads to further confusion and wounding. Solitude is for focusing on God.

32. Introspection is pervasive in our self-absorbed culture. I gain true understanding by waiting on God, listening for what he would say to me.

33. Solitude and silence foster clarity. Particles slowly settle after clear water is stirred. Busyness dissipates as the soul becomes still.

CHAPTER TEN

How to Spend Time in Solitude

A Day, or Hours, or

Let's move one step further in our exploration of the practice of solitude and silence and discover how we might spend a day there.

1. Preparing to spend a day in solitude and silence, we encounter principles that can be applied to shorter periods—even hours or minutes.

2. In biblical rhythms the new day begins at sundown. In Jewish practice the Sabbath is ushered in by the Friday evening meal.

3. A helpful practice in shaping an orderly life: use the period after the evening meal and before going to bed to prepare for the next day.

4. Prepare for your day with God. Go to bed early and sleep until rested. A rested body supports coming present to God and hearing him well.

5. Unless sleep has been disturbed, we awake in solitude and silence and want to remain there. Sleep gives welcome relief from busyness and noise.

6. We pre-select a place to spend our day that is sheltered from intrusions. Ideally we can awake and move to this location without interruptions.

7. We prepare this space. It is important that we enjoy being there. An extra cup of coffee or a snack for later on might be helpful.

8. We may choose to spend all or part of our day in nature. Solitude and nature go well together. Nature is restful—it is not rebelling against its Creator.

9. Two movements of the soul take place in solitude. The soul:
   • abstains from what is toxic
   • engages with what restores

10. We begin our time in solitude with abstinence. The soul must first be emptied, cleansed. The time will come for engagement, receiving, filling.

11. We fast from phone/email/internet. If we are checking messages, our soul is no longer in solitude. But during engagement, worship music can be enriching.

12. We don't bring work with us. If we are working on our "to do" list, our soul is no longer in solitude. This time is my gift to God—and to myself!

13. We practice doing nothing—itself a major discipline or achievement. Many find the very idea challenging, so deeply has busyness shaped us.

14. As I enter more deeply into rest, I grow in my awareness of the condition of my soul. Practice expands my ability to go deeper into silence.

15. Abstinence gradually prepares me for engagement—for receiving. The time may come to undertake other spiritual practices such as study.

16. An area of personal need may have been clarified for me. I may want to seek the Lord in other practices like meditation, prayer, study, journaling.

17. Solitude and healing are closely related. In solitude I gain insight into my brokenness, but I also experience the power of my Father's unconditional love.

18. We ask the Spirit to guide. We rely on him. There is no right or wrong way to "do" solitude. We are just "hanging out" with our Father. He teaches us.

19. We consider what rhythm we want solitude and silence to have in our lives:
    • a daily practice?
    • weekly?
    • monthly?
    • annually?
    • We make plans.

20. What is impossible to do today, or later this week, becomes easily doable by planning ahead. I take responsibility, schedule, and make arrangements.

21. Solitude and silence comfort the lonely. Some fear solitude will increase loneliness. But in the silences of God, I experience that I am never alone.

22. Rising very early in the morning, while it was still dark, he departed and went out to a desolate place, and there he prayed (Mark 1:35).

CHAPTER ELEVEN

Prayer

Being with God and Interacting with Him
About All We Are Doing Together

1. Jesus lived a life of prayer. He often withdrew from activity to be with his Father. In his humanity, prayer was the source of his strength.

2. Jesus taught a life of prayer. He formed prayer in his disciples by example and teaching. Prayer is foundational to being his follower.

3. The apostles lived and taught a life of prayer. It permeates the New Testament. They learned prayer from Jesus. Prayer empowered the Church's birth and growth.

4. Examine Judeo-Christian history. You will find no one who walked with God or accomplished great things for him who was not a man or woman of prayer.

5. What is prayer? Prayer is interacting with God. I talk to him. I make requests. I listen to hear what he is saying to me. Prayer is

two-way communication.

6. There is something special about prayers we form using our own words. What father does not love to hear honoring words from his own child?

7. But we do not know how to pray. We need the Holy Spirit to help us (Rom. 8:26). The disciples asked Jesus to teach them how to pray (Lk. 11:1).

8. We also learn much about how to pray through prayers that have stood the test of time among God's people down through the centuries.

9. The prayers of David (and others) in the Psalms have shaped the worship and prayers of our spiritual forefathers and mothers for millennia.

10. The prayers of Jesus and his followers, found in the New Testament, laid the initial foundation for Christian worship and prayer.

11. We have received a rich heritage in the prayers of Christian history, formed by ones who walked with God, representing every Christian tradition.

12. Unaided, we can pray amiss. The heart may be innocent, but the understandings which form prayers may be wrong—even spiritually dark.

13. Scripture includes repetition in prayer (Ps. 136). Repetition supports meditation, facilitating hearing God more thoroughly and accurately.

14. Some equate prayer only with intercession. Intercessory prayer is certainly essential! Here we will focus on prayer as it relates to living in the Presence.

15. Prayer is primary in practicing God's Presence. To learn how to live in God's Presence continually, we must learn how to pray continually.

16. The biblical directive to pray without ceasing seems unattainable (1 Thess. 5:17). But it is a command. Let's ask the Lord to teach us how.

17. "Rejoice always, pray without ceasing, give thanks in all circumstances" (1 Thess. 5:16-18). Rejoicing, praying, giving thanks are to fill our lives.

18. *Perfection* is different from *maturity*. We will never be perfect in praying without ceasing, but we can increasingly mature toward it.

19. Jesus directs us to abide in him (Jn. 15:5). He said apart from him we could do nothing. "To abide" means "to remain." Remain for how long?

20. The Scriptures say we are to be filled with the Spirit (Eph. 5:18). For how long? Is this just a one-off experience? Or a way of life?

21. Praying without ceasing, abiding in Christ and being filled with the Spirit all point to one reality—living in continual communion with God.

22. This is the condition for which we were created. We can re-learn this. But the old life must be brought to the cross that a new life may be formed.

23. When we try to pray without ceasing, our mind wanders. Keeping our mind on anything involves learning to bring our mind continually back to it.

24. To learn prayer as a lifestyle I practice shortening the intervals when my thoughts are not on God. I look for ways to bring my

thoughts back more often.

25. There is no "right" way to shorten the intervals between returning my thoughts to God, but history has many examples from which I can learn.

26. In New Testament times the liturgical day in Judaism included set hours for prayer (Acts 3:1). Cornelius, a Gentile, prayed them (Acts 10:30).

27. Cornelius was a Roman centurion, an army officer with 100 men under him. He had a busy schedule, but he "prayed continuously" (Acts 10:2).

28. "Seven times a day I praise you" guided early Christian houses of prayer (monasteries) to set hours of prayer day and night (Ps. 119:164).

29. Historically seven hours of prayer have been used by Christian communities: upon rising, 6AM, 9AM, noon, 3PM, 6PM and before retiring.

30. How can I develop a lifestyle of prayer? 1) Start with one prayer time a day. It can be short! Connect with God.

31. In learning any discipline, we start where we are. Don't overdo it. Attempting too much too soon will be counterproductive. Let habits of prayer develop naturally.

32. The more we are with God, the deeper our desire to be with him will grow. Once one prayer time per day is established, 2) add a second one.

33. Two prayer times a day might look like one in the morning and one in the evening. In time, 3) a third one might be added at noontime.

34. A next step may be 4) to set the timer on our watch or phone to sound every so often—once an hour? Hearing it, we pause to speak briefly, quietly to the Lord.

35. As I write this, my watch timer is sounding every five minutes. I pause for a five-second prayer. I don't feel interrupted; I feel empowered.

36. Each of us can discover unique ways to return our thoughts to God throughout the day for a five-second prayer. Being with God will be transformative.

CHAPTER TWELVE

Prayers That Can Be Prayed in Five Seconds (or Less)

Toward Moment by Moment Communion

1. How can we pray throughout the day while negotiating the responsibilities of life? We need ways of repeatedly returning our thoughts to God.

2. Most of us can hit the pause button in the midst of normal activities for five seconds or less. Below are prayers that can be prayed in that time frame.

3. Remember—prayer is more than asking. It is communicating with God. It is practicing his Presence. We speak to him. We listen for what he might say.

4. There is also worshipful prayer. We declare before God truths about him. We praise him. We thank him. We are simply with him.

5. This list of prayers is only a beginning. In case it is helpful, there is one for each day of the month.

1) Our Father, who art in heaven, hallowed be your name (Mt. 6:9).
2) Lord Jesus, teach me to pray (Lk. 11:1).
3) Come Holy Spirit.
4) Thy kingdom come, thy will be done, on earth as it is in heaven (Mt. 6:10).
5) Lord, have mercy. Christ, have mercy. Lord, have mercy.
6) Holy Spirit, I rely on you (Gal. 5:16).
7) Create in me a clean heart, O God (Ps. 51:10).
8) Lord Jesus, teach me how to abide in you 24/7 (Jn. 15:4).
9) Holy Spirit, lead me in prayer (Rom. 8:26).
10) My soul magnifies the Lord (Lk. 1:46).
11) Blessed is he who comes in the name of the Lord (Ps. 118:26).
12) Come Holy Spirit; fill my heart (my soul, mind, body, relationships).
13) My soul waits for the Lord more than watchmen for the morning (Ps. 130:6a).
14) Lord Jesus, give me your grace to forgive my enemy (Lk. 6:27-28).
15) Glory be to the Father, and to the Son, and to the Holy Spirit.
16) Give us this day our daily bread (Mt. 6:11).
17) Lord, you make known to me the path of life. Thank you (Ps. 16:11).
18) Father, in your Presence there is fullness of joy (Ps. 16:11).
19) For God alone my soul waits in silence (Ps. 62:1).
20) Lord, I can do nothing of spiritual benefit without you (Jn. 15:5).
21) Unless the Lord builds the house, those who build it labor in vain (Ps. 127:1).
22) Lord Jesus, please heal me (Lk. 5:17).
23) Lord, I do not know the way. But I know you. You are the Way (Jn. 14:6).
24) The Lord is my shepherd; I shall not want (Ps. 23:1).
25) Lord, how majestic is your name in all the earth (Ps. 8:1).
26) Lord Jesus, grant me your peace (Jn. 14:27).
27) Search me, O God, and know my heart (Ps. 139:23a).
28) Heavenly Father (Lord Jesus … Holy Spirit), thank you for your love.
29) Heavenly Father (Lord Jesus … Holy Spirit), I love you.
30) Heavenly Father (Lord Jesus … Holy Spirit), I trust you.

6. These are only to get us started. Soon we will be formulating prayers using our own words to express what is on our hearts at a given moment.

7. We might set the timer on our watch or phone to sound at pre-chosen intervals. Hearing the sound, we pause for a few seconds—and pray silently.

8. In learning to practice God's Presence, there is another way we can use five second prayers. It can be called the "three times four" (3 x 4) approach.

9. The "three" here refers to the three Persons of the Trinity. We pray first to the Father, then to the Son, then to the Holy Spirit.

10. The "four" refers to how many times we are going to pray our prayer to each Person.

11. Why four? No special reason—it just seems to work well. If another rhythm works better for you, by all means use it.

12. So, for example, we could pray, "Father, I love you. Father, I love you. Father, I love you. Father, I love you."

13. Then we could pray four times to the Son. We may choose to use the same words, or we may choose different ones.

14. Then we could pray four times to the Holy Spirit.

15. Of course we may pray each prayer less than four times, or more. The more deeply a habit is formed the more freedom we find to deviate from it.

16. So we might pray, "Father, I love you. Lord Jesus, I love you. Holy Spirit, I love you."

17. The point of course is not the numbers, or even the prayer. It is

learning habits of coming into the Lord's Presence and remaining there.

18. The inner life is opened up to God. He is invited in. This will surely in time yield beautiful fruit: peace, insight, healing, meaning, transformation, joy.

19. And then there is the quiet listening for the words our Father may be wanting to speak to us.

20. I find "three times four" praying to be a wonderful way to pray myself to sleep.

21. And now a longer prayer which embraces much of what we have been learning in *Maturing toward Wholeness in the Inner Life:*

Lord Jesus, I bring my sin, and the guilt and destructive behaviors it has caused, to you on the cross. Thank you Lord! On the cross you made provision for my guilt to be removed, my wounds to be healed and the power of sin in my behavior to be broken. Lead me now into the faith, expressed by obedience, which enables me to access this provision of your grace.

CHAPTER THIRTEEN

With All Your Heart

Create in me a clean heart, O God, and renew a right spirit
within me. Psalm 51:10

1. In Mark 12:29-31 Jesus refers to five components of the human person—heart, soul, mind, strength (body), and social relationships (love of neighbor).

2. Each component in me has been damaged by sin—the sin I have committed, and the sin all around me in family and society. Each must be re-formed.

3. In this and the next four chapters I have been significantly influenced by Dallas Willard's *Renovation of the Heart*. I am deeply grateful.

4. What did Jesus mean by "heart"? Willard's understanding:

   Now, when we set aside contemporary prejudices, and carefully examine these two great sources [the Judeo-Christian and the

Greek, the biblical and the classical] I believe it will become clear that "heart", "spirit", and "will" (or their equivalents) are words that refer to one and the same thing, the same fundamental component of the person (*Renovation of the Heart*, p. 29).

5. For our purposes here, we will concentrate on understanding the heart as referring to my will, my intention, my choices.

6. Of all the components of my person, I have most direct control of my will or choices—more than my soul, mind, body or social relationships.

7. It may seem that I have more control of my body. But I don't control many bodily functions, and most of the ones I do control require my will to act first.

8. It may seem that I have more control of my mind. But thoughts and emotions regularly come which I did not choose or intend. I must choose how to respond.

9. I can "choose" what I intend, though I cannot always "do" what I intend. This introduces to us the distinction between "will" and "will-power."

10. Choosing what I intend to do or be is a function of my will. Ability to do what I intend to do or be is a function of the condition of my inner life.

11. Of course the ability to do what I intend also often depends on external circumstances. Most external circumstances are beyond my control.

12. Relying on "will-power" to behave the way I intend often leads to defeat. Relying on Christ in everything results in becoming a new kind of person.

13. Following the teachings of Jesus gradually transforms my inner life.

I don't do it. The Holy Spirit does it. But I must choose it.

14. Freedom to make my own choices lies at the core of my personhood, my individuality, my creativity, my human dignity. It expresses the image of God in me.

15. God is free to make his own choices. He created me free to make my own choices. But caution! I am not free to avoid the consequences of my choices.

16. My choices, more than anything else, are what is uniquely me. Decisions I am making day by day are forming the person I am becoming—forever.

17. The freedom to choose gives human beings the ability to create. Our Creator created us creative—like he is.

18. Nothing violates a person more than attempting to take away the freedom to make his or her own choices. Observe the reactions of small children.

19. God took a risk when he created us free. But it was essential to his intent. He was creating beings who bore his image and with whom he could share intimacy.

20. Love requires freedom to choose. Though expressed outwardly, the decision to love first forms inwardly. Love cannot be forced; the heart must choose it.

21. Worship requires freedom to choose. Jesus said God is seeking worshippers (Jn. 4:23). Worship cannot be forced; the heart must choose it.

22. The human person—heart, soul, mind, body, social relation-ships—is badly damaged. Sin did this. Jesus renews us by his grace. But we must choose it.

23. God will not force himself on a person. He values us too highly. To violate our will would de-humanize us. He calls, offers himself, and awaits our response.

24. This offers insight as to how to relate with others. We do not try to force our will on them. We respect their God-given freedom to make their own choices.

25. My heart must direct the re-making of my person. "Keep your heart with all vigilance, for from it flow the springs of life" (Prov. 4:23).

26. But my heart has also been damaged by sin. It too must be re-formed. I can intend to rely on God, but I find that my intention fluctuates.

27. I must intend that my intention be re-trained. I learn to habitually:
    • repent of my failures
    • return my heart to reliance on God (faith)

28. Only the Holy Spirit, not the force of my willpower, can re-form my heart. Only I, by my choices, can give him permission to do so (Ps. 139:23-24).

29. Both repenting and re-setting my will are repetitive processes. A child learns to walk by falling down and getting up—again and again.

30. I learn not to be de-railed by discouragement. One look at self; ten looks at Jesus! No matter how many times I fail, he never gives up on me.

31. Freedom to choose is essential for healthy submission to God-established authorities. Heart submission cannot be forced or demanded.

32. Demanding submission violates the will and triggers anger. God

does not force submission. He invites us to submit to his love and wisdom for our own benefit.

33. My anger is activated when my will is crossed. I feel violated and want to retaliate. But retaliating can wound me more than the original offense.

34. Choosing to rely on God to right the wrong releases me from anger and heals me. Jesus teaches me how to do this in apprenticeship to him.

35. Many are surprised to learn that God actually submits to us! How so? He chooses not to override our choices even when they are grievous to him.

36. Only by choosing to submit to another person do we allow that person to love us. Only by choosing to submit to God do we allow him to transform us.

37. God saves all who allow him to do so. If I refuse, with great sadness, he honors my decision. Only my own choices can separate me from him.

38. "You will seek me and find me, when you seek me with all your heart" (Jer. 29:13).

39. Jesus: "Blessed are the pure in heart, for they shall see God" (Mt. 5:8).

CHAPTER FOURTEEN

With All Your Soul

The LORD is my shepherd…he restores my soul. Psalm 23:1,3

1. In considering the five components of the human person, which Jesus referred to in Mark 12:29-31, we now come to the soul. It too must be re-formed.

2. Again, Dallas Willard offers a definition in *Renovation of the Heart* that is extremely insightful:

   What is running your life at any moment is your soul. Not external circumstances, or your thoughts, or your intentions, or even your feelings, but your soul. The soul is that aspect of your whole being that *correlates*, *integrates*, and *enlivens* everything going on in the various dimensions of the self. It is the life center of the human being. It regulates whatever is occurring in each of those dimensions and how they interact with each other and respond to surrounding events in the overall governance of your life. The soul is "deep" in the sense of being basic or foundational and also in the sense that it lies almost totally beyond conscious awareness (*Renovation of the Heart*, p. 199).

3. Jesus teaches me to love God with all my soul. If my soul lies almost beyond awareness, how do I gain insight into it? Let's look at some biblical descriptions.

4. Biblical information about the soul is rich and plentiful.
   • The soul worships (Lk. 1:46).
   • The soul longs for God (Ps. 42:1).
   • The soul can be troubled (Ps. 6:3).
   • The soul can be distraught (Ps. 88:3).
   • The soul can be cast down (Ps. 42:5).
   • The soul can be quieted (Ps. 131:2).
   • The soul can be consoled (Ps. 94:19).
   • The soul can desire evil (Ps. 10:3).
   • The soul can desire good (Ps. 119:20).
   • The soul can be sorrowful (Mt. 26:38).
   • The soul can find rest (Mt. 11:29).
   • The soul can be strengthened (Acts 14:22).
   • The soul can be kept blameless (1 Thess. 5:23).
   • The soul is saved from wickedness by God's word (Jm. 1:21).
   • The soul is revived through God's law (Ps. 19:7).
   • The soul is preserved by relying on God (Heb. 10:39).
   • The soul finds an anchor in God and his promises (Heb. 6:19).
   • The soul needs guarding (Ps. 25:20).
   • The soul waits for God (Ps. 130:5-6).
   • The soul can be humbled (Ps. 69:10).
   • The soul can be embittered (Ps. 73:21).
   • The soul has the capacity to bless (Gen. 27:1-4).
   • The soul gives me counsel (Ps. 13:2).
   • The soul can be deceived (Lk. 12:19-20).
   • The soul is the source of obedience (Ps. 119:167).
   • God has a soul (Ps. 11:5).

5. If my soul is almost beyond awareness, how do I personally connect with it? One way is the practice of solitude. In solitude I discover that I have a soul.

6. If my soul is almost beyond awareness, a major way of gaining

insight into it is through intuition. But I am always careful to test my intuition by the Bible.

7. To cultivate spiritual re-formation, I must understand my soul and care for it. It is important to know its needs and respond to them.

8. **My soul needs creativity**—that which I produce and that which comes from others. My Creator created me creative.

9. The damaged soul is offered comfort—and healing—in the presence of ennobling art in music, painting, writing, architecture, and other forms.

10. Perhaps the greatest art we can encounter is nature—the artwork of the supreme Creator.

11. **My soul needs silence.** God is active, and he has spoken. But there are also the healing silences of God. "For God alone my soul waits in silence" (Ps. 62:1a).

12. Silence offers the soul the option to withdraw from distractions which do not heal, and can wound further, and to soak in God's Presence.

13. **My soul needs rootedness.** Being rooted in an environment of committed relationships is essential to my well-being. I am incomplete without others.

14. God designed this need to be met in family and church. But just as I have been damaged by sin, so have others in my family and church fellowship.

15. As I mature toward wholeness, Jesus equips me to be an agent of healing. I learn not to demand that others meet my needs; I focus on meeting their needs.

16. "Place" is important to rootedness. Where we were born, or the

region from which our family comes, are foundational to our identity. "Home" is a soul word.

17. The soul's need for place can be seen in other ways. For example, in the family someone may have a favorite room, or lay claim to a certain chair.

18. **My soul needs meaning.** When life lacks meaning, only boredom and will-power remain. The soul cannot endure meaninglessness for long.

19. An empty soul is the consequence of living apart from God. Only in and with God does the human person find enduring meaning.

20. The empty soul seeks meaning in that which is superficial. That which is superficial cannot meet a need that is deep. It only offers temporary escape.

21. The empty soul may look for meaning in that which is evil. What is evil only damages the soul further.

22. The needs of the human soul are fully and forever satisfied by being relationally reconciled with its Creator through the cross of Christ.

23. **My soul needs order.** Those who create chaos around them are expressing chaotic souls. A life of obedience to God is orderly, peaceful, structured.

24. God is a God of order. He created an orderly universe. "All things should be done decently and in order" (1 Cor. 14:40).

25. One of God's provisions for our need for order is his law. "The law of the Lord is perfect, reviving the soul" (Ps. 19:7a).

26. There can be confusion among Christians about God's law. The law never claims to justify us before God. Nothing can do that except Christ's cross.

27. God's law expresses his nature and his ways. It is his precious gift to mankind. It offers insight and order for life in grace.

28. It has been said that God's law is not the *source* of righteousness, but it is the *course* of righteousness.

29. Jesus: "Until heaven and earth pass away, not an iota, not a dot, will pass from the Law until all is accomplished" (Mt. 5:18b).

30. **My soul needs God's Presence.** I am created for God's Presence as a fish is created for water. Away from God, my soul grows empty, then chaotic.

31. As I learn how to live in God's Presence my soul is restored. "My soul waits for the Lord more than watchmen for the morning" (Ps. 130:6a).

32. How can I understand the difference between my heart and my soul? I have far-reaching, often immediate, influence over my choices (heart).

33. Influence over my soul is indirect. The condition of my soul is progressively shaped by—becomes an expression of—the choices of my heart.

34. As I intend with my heart to rely on God and live in his Presence, the Spirit progressively re-shapes my soul. My soul matures toward Christlikeness.

35. As Christlikeness forms in my soul it further influences the actions of my heart, mind (thoughts and emotions), body, and social relationships.

36. The most basic issue of my Christian life is not my behavior. Good fruit requires a good tree. My behavior expresses the kind of person I am becoming.

37. Over time my soul takes on a certain character—predictable ways in which I will choose, think, feel, respond bodily, and relate.

38. The soul does not remain static. Each person's soul has been formed and continues to be formed. It can also be re-formed.

39. "This is just the kind of person I am." Really? Believing I cannot change only suggests that I have been unable to change by relying on myself.

40. Believing I cannot change denies the Gospel. It is dismissive of God's promises and power. "If anyone is in Christ, he is a new creation" (2 Cor. 5:17).

41. I make choices. My choices lead to behaviors. These behaviors have consequences. I respond to these consequences. All this forms my soul.

42. Obedience to God re-forms my soul. Obedience requires heart choices and bodily actions. What I do with my body affects my soul.

43. A soul formed apart from God becomes increasingly fragmented, disordered, chaotic. The likelihood that I will harm myself and others increases.

44. The soul will be shaken in crises—illness, financial loss, relational failure, death of a loved one—when it is only relying on itself (Ps. 62:1-2).

45. The Bible calls the condition of a fragmented, chaotic, destructive soul "death"—the state of every soul apart from Christ (Rom. 1:18-31).

46. God at times judges sin by choosing not to intervene. He lets man experience the consequences of evil choices and behaviors emanating from ruined souls.

47. We may bring God's judgment on ourselves. We may choose it. But we can change our choices—repentance! In sending his Son, God invites us to do so.

48. Good News (the Gospel)—souls can be re-formed—brought from death to life. We have not been left in the hell of slavery to destructive habits and behaviors.

49. A soul centered in God comes to rest. It has returned home. My whole being, in spite of what is going on around me, finds order and peace (Mt. 11:29).

50. A soul not centered in God remains fragmented. It can't find its way home. It is lost. One's whole being trends toward chaos and unwanted behaviors.

51. We read almost daily of politicians, athletes, executives, entertainers, religious leaders who are self-destructing due to disordered, chaotic souls.

52. "Bless the Lord, O my soul, and all that is within me, bless his holy name" (Ps. 103:1). Come, Holy Spirit. Fill my soul!

CHAPTER FIFTEEN

With All Your Mind – Thoughts

May the mind of Christ, my Savior, grow in me from day to day, by his love and power transforming all I do and say. *

1. In considering the five components of the human person Jesus referred to in Mark 12:29-31, we now come to the mind. It too must be re-formed.

2. It is helpful to view the mind as being composed of thoughts and emotions. These are closely related. We look at emotions in the next chapter.

3. The first step in my re-formation is intention—an orientation of the heart. I choose to intend to learn from Jesus how to become the kind of person he is.

4. My first step in implementing this intention is to choose where I will place my thoughts. Jesus teaches me to live with my thoughts centered in God.

*Adapted from the song "May the Mind of Christ my Savior" by Kate B. Wilkinso

5. At first, thinking about God all the time seems strange, hard, unappealing. This reflects the extent of the damage sin has caused within me.

6. I am created for life in God's Presence. To live in God's Presence I live with him in my thoughts. This leads to peace, purity, insight, and overall well-being.

7. I need help in becoming able to do this. I turn to Jesus—the Master Teacher (Jn. 13:13). I become his apprentice. He teaches me by his Spirit.

8. The entire Bible teaches me to center my thoughts in God. How am I to think about the Bible? How did Jesus think about the Bible?

9. Jesus viewed the Bible as authoritative. He didn't feel the need to defend it. He took it at face value and lived by it. It was the foundation of his teachings.

10. Jesus to the Sadducees: "Is this not the reason you are wrong, because you know neither the Scriptures nor the power of God" (Mk. 12:24b).

11. We have two kinds of thoughts:
    • analytical thoughts
    • imaginative or intuitive thoughts
    • Both are God-given; both have their place.

12. My car breaks down on a deserted road. What am I going to do now? My God-given capacity to think analytically will be extremely useful!

13. But analysis, so valuable when used appropriately, has limits. Large areas of reality can only be accessed intuitively.

14. How do I know that a sunset is beautiful? That I love my family? That I want to study a certain subject? That God is real and I have met him?

15. Much truth loses meaning when analyzed. Some classical writers equated truth with beauty. Beauty's essence is inaccessible to analysis.

16. Jesus knew this. He taught primarily to the intuitive. Why? The integrating theme of his teaching was an Unseen Kingdom. Its realities must be intuited.

17. Jewish leaders asked Jesus to explain the source of his authority. He asked them to explain the source of John the Baptist's authority (Mt. 21:23).

18. The source of Jesus' authority was God's Unseen kingdom. Its qualities cannot be discovered scientifically or accessed analytically. They must be intuited.

19. Jesus: "Have you believed because you have seen me? Blessed are those who have not seen and yet have believed" (Jn. 20:29). God's kingdom is unseen.

20. Symbols are vehicles of intuitive communication. Effective leaders know how to use them. They convey meaning directly to the imagination.

21. The power of symbols is *beyond words*. Jesus used them extensively. To grasp the depth of Jesus' teachings the intuition must be fully engaged.

22. Jesus: "I am the bread of life." "I am the door." "I am the way." "Come to me and drink." "I and the Father are one." The meanings must be intuited.

23. Meanings in Jesus' parables must be intuited. The kingdom of heaven is like treasure in a field. A wise man sold all he had to buy the field (Mt. 13:44).

24. Caution! The imaginative mind can also connect with what is unhealthy or spiritually dark. Conclusions must always be tested by Scripture.

25. A plate and chalice are before me as I write. I pause to look at them and pray. Jesus gave us symbols of communion when he invited us to remember him.

26. Church history is rich with symbols that inform the mind about God: cross, water, bread, wine, oil, paintings, icons. Their power must be rediscovered.

27. Here mind and soul connect. As the intuitive mind dwells on the beauty of God through the use of symbols, the soul is nourished.

28. Many assume truth can only be discovered analytically. They tirelessly analyze themselves and God. The result? God often seems far away—unreal.

29. We can reach a point where we *live in our heads*. We become compulsively analytical—cut off from ourselves and the Presence of the Resurrected One.

30. Living in our heads further wounds us. We experience tension, uncertainty and striving rather than peace, healing and wholeness in God's Presence.

31. Many believe we can grow closer to God by analyzing the Bible. Analyzing the Bible has its place. But we grow closer to God by living in his Presence.

32. Beliefs develop from worldview. Worldview is based on assumptions. The assumptions with which analysis begins will shape the conclusions analysis draws.

33. Many focus on the doctrine of salvation. What is biblical salvation? Only removing my guilt? What about breaking sin's power in my behavior? (Rom. 6-8)

34. "As he who called you is holy, you also be holy in all your conduct, since it is written, 'You shall be holy, for I am holy'" (1 Pt. 1:15-16).

35. Other doctrines inform our understanding of salvation. There is the doctrine of God. Who is he? What does he intend for man? What is his purpose in history?

36. "In the beginning, God created the heavens and the earth" (Gen. 1:1). Understanding that God is my Creator is foundational to my re-formation.

37. Sin left all creation "in bondage to corruption" (Rom. 8:21). In salvation God is restoring all things. "Behold, I am making all things new" (Rev. 21:5).

38. Of the "all things" God is making new, the human person is primary. "If anyone is in Christ, he is a new creation" (2 Cor. 5:17a).

39. A biblical and time-tested practice in living with my thoughts on God is meditating on Scripture.

40. Psalm 1:2 describes the man who is blessed: "His delight is in the law of the Lord, and on his law he meditates day and night."

41. An effective way to meditate on Scripture is to memorize it. Memorizing phrases or verses is good; memorizing complete passages is even better.

42. If one is wondering where to start, consider beginning with Jesus' teaching in John 13-17 and Paul's teaching in Romans 6-8.

43. So we pray: "Come Holy Spirit. Fill my thoughts. Fill my analytical thoughts. Shape my worldview by the Bible that my reasoning may lead me to truth."

44. We also pray: "Come Holy Spirit. Fill my intuitive thoughts. Give insight that can come only from you. Protect my thoughts from what is soulish or dark."

CHAPTER SIXTEEN

With All Your Mind – Emotions

The fruit of the Spirit is love, joy, peace, patience, kindness, goodness, faithfulness, gentleness, self-control. Galatians 5:22-23a

1. In considering the five components of the human person outlined by Jesus in Mark 12:29-31, we now seek further understanding of the mind.

2. We are viewing the mind as being composed of thoughts and emotions. In this chapter we explore human emotions. They too must be re-formed.

3. God has emotions. The Scriptures describe characteristics of God which are accompanied by emotions.
   • God is love (1 Jn. 4:8).
   • God knows joy (Neh. 8:10).
   • God creates peace (Heb. 13:20).
   • God exercises patience (Rom. 2:4).
   • God is kind (Ps. 145:17).
   • God is good (Ps. 107:1).

- God is faithful (Ps. 31:5).
- God is gentle (2 Sam. 22:36).
- God can be pleased (1 Kings 3:10).
- God can be grieved (Gen. 6:6).
- God can become angry (2 Sam. 6:7).
- God can lay down his anger (Amos 7:1-3).
- God is forgiving (Ps. 86:5).
- God initiates reconciliation with his enemies (Rom. 5:10-11).
- God shows mercy (Ps. 103:4).

4. Human beings are created in God's image. We too have emotions. God designed us for expressing our emotions in ways that are healthy, beautiful, delightful.

5. The fruit which characterizes the Holy Spirit (Gal. 5:22-23a) gives insight into God's emotions. The Spirit forms these in people who allow him to do so.

6. The components of this one fruit (singular) are best viewed as characteristics of one who is walking with God. They are accompanied by emotions.

7. Take love for example. Love is more than a feeling. It is a condition, a quality of relationship that one person chooses toward another. Feelings accompany it.

8. Some of our emotions may not be in the condition God intended for them. Sin damages. Wounded emotions can be very strong and frightfully uncontrollable.

9. In our current cultural environment in the western world, emotions are considered to be valid simply because they exist.

10. If I feel it, I have the right to express it. How dare you even suggest that I don't have the right to express what I am feeling!

11. This idea is rooted in a belief system that sees humans as autonomous. There are no absolutes except what man, beginning from himself, arbitrarily selects.

12. It lacks any acknowledgement of lurking dangers. Acting autonomously can feel good in the moment, but can result in painful damage to me and others.

13. Contrast this with the belief system Jesus taught: Man is created by God to be like him. Some choices result in life functioning well; some choices lead to harm.

14. Not everything I desire is good for me. To successfully navigate life, I must learn how to order my desires under the wisdom, governance, and goodness of God.

15. The engine of my car is designed—created—for oil. If I keep the oil topped up, the engine will function well. If I allow the oil to drain out, I will ruin the engine.

16. It is my car. I can do with it whatever I want! True enough. But if I choose to treat it in ways for which it was not designed, I will damage it.

17. So it is with my emotions. God is the manufacturer of my person. If I choose to act in ways contrary to how I was designed, I will damage myself—and others.

18. How can we seek deeper insight into our emotions? In Matthew 5:21-48 Jesus teaches about seven behaviors to avoid. Each negatively impacts emotional health.

19. **Anger.** My anger is aroused when my will is crossed. I feel a strong desire to hit back. But I can learn that I am not under compulsion to give in to every feeling.

20. Jesus placed anger in the category with murder and contempt. (Mt. 5:21-22) All three are behaviors of violence toward others.

21. Anger negatively marks all who experience it—perpetrator, victim, bystander. It is not pleasant to be around someone venting anger.

22. There are better strategies for achieving my desired ends than anger. Whatever I try to achieve by anger can be better accomplished without it.

23. We were not created for anger. It is death-producing rather than life-giving. The ways of Jesus are different.

24. So what do I do with my anger? Stuff it? No! It will only erupt in an unguarded moment. God's way is not to suppress harmful emotions—but to transform them.

25. **Contempt.** We treat another person with contempt when we speak about him, or to him, or relate to him, in ways that dishonor, despise or dehumanize him.

26. Contempt typically begins with speech. We call others "fools" or "idiots" or something worse. We work to find words that will inflict the greatest hurt.

27. Hateful speech gives permission for hateful acts. Here are the roots of racism, slavery, misogyny, ethnic cleansing and hatred of those who are the *others*.

28. Contemptuous speech can become "normal" in political life. Living with Jesus, we become the kind of people who can discuss differing political views respectfully.

29. When we speak of a political opponent with contempt, one thing can be said with certainty—we did not learn to talk that way by being with Jesus.

30. **Sexual lust.** God created us so that a man and a woman could share a one-of-a-kind unique intimacy, and could express this physically (Chapter 19).

31. God further designed us so that the physical, sexual expression of this one-of-a-kind intimacy would result in beautiful, honoring emotions for both persons.

32. Bodily intimacy (sexual activity) apart from intimacy of persons (unique, shared commitment), violates the intent of the Creator and those who engage in it.

33. Sexual activity that is only physical can indeed generate strong emotions. But it is without integrity. It cheapens and damages persons who engage in it.

34. The emotions it generates are short-lived and ultimately unsatisfying. They can transition quickly into contempt, even hatred (2 Sam. 13:14).

35. What is superficial cannot meet needs that are deep. Sexual behavior outside of authentic, committed, mutual intimacy of persons wounds the soul.

36. **Divorce.** We must think and speak of divorce with tenderness and compassion. Some among us have experienced it, and the wounds it leaves behind.

37. A fundamental violation in divorce is personal abandonment. The deepest of all human relationships is being severed. People are leaving each other.

38. Those considering divorce do well to call "time-out" and seek help. Divorce is never a good option. Sadly, at times, it can be the better of two unfortunate choices.

39. The circle of those affected goes well beyond the two whose marriage is ending. Divorce reveals how broadly we are inter-related—children, family, friends.

40. Damaged emotions involved in divorce may take years to heal. But Jesus is a specialist in healing! Personal crises of all kinds beckon us to go deeper with God.

41. **Oaths.** What was wrong with swearing oaths as practiced in Jesus' day? There were two issues, arrogant presumption and verbal manipulation (Mt. 5:33-37).

42. In our 21st century world we daily encounter the idea that we can control our life circumstances. "If you can imagine it, you can do it." Really?

43. Jesus: "And do not take an oath by your head, for you cannot make one hair white or black." Claiming to control what is beyond my control is living in unreality.

44. I am not self-determined, self-sufficient or all-powerful. I control neither the external nor internal circumstances of my life; only God does (Jm. 4:13-15).

45. The next issue is verbal manipulation. The motivation for swearing oaths was to add weight to what was being said—to override the judgment of the hearers.

46. God doesn't manipulate or override. He speaks directly, truthfully, respectfully, and allows us to reach our own conclusions. "Yes" means "yes"; "no" means "no."

47. Of course we must make commitments—life does not work without them. We do so with humility, owning our limitations, acknowledging our need for God's help.

48. Marriage vows are a prime example. Hanna and I ended our marriage vows with "May the Lord help me." We know we need God's help to keep our promises.

49. Also legitimate is testifying under oath in a judicial process. This establishes a legal basis for what is said. Its purpose is to protect against verbal manipulation.

50. **Retaliation.** When we respond to an offense, real or imagined, by wanting to retaliate, we assume a role God has not given us—the role of judge.

51. To try to justify myself—to right every wrong—is unworkable. It leaves me frustrated. It wounds me further. The way of Jesus: I leave pay-back to my Father.

52. Only God has a fully accurate view of the wrong. What really happened? Who is to blame? Only God can judge with the proper balance of truth and mercy.

53. **Love of enemies.** How can I possibly love my enemies? Not by greater *will-power*. I must become a new kind of person—the kind of person who forgives.

54. How do I become the kind of person who forgives (see Chapter 20)? The answer: I become the kind of person Jesus is.

55. Initial steps to becoming the kind of person who forgives:
    • Forgiveness never denies or minimizes the wrong.
    • Forgiveness faces the truth without deciding judgment.
    • Forgiveness leaves it to God to judge the "bad guys" and assign punishment.
    • Forgiveness results in the healing and freeing of the one feeling wronged.

56. How do I pursue the re-formation of my emotions? Let's look

again at the fruit of the Holy Spirit and its components (Gal. 5:22-23a).

57. These components are best seen as conditions accompanied by emotions. I pursue the condition, for example love. In time the emotions follow.

58. The most direct ways I have to regulate my emotions are choices as to where I will place my thoughts. I practice the Presence. I locate my thoughts in Scripture.

59. What do I do with painful emotions? Jesus' way is not to block them out or suppress them. Any relief this may yield will be short lived.

60. God's way is to heal painful emotions. Practicing his Presence, I bring my pain to Jesus on the cross. In my imaginative mind I *see* him dying there for me.

61. I ask him to take my pain and administer his healing. He died for my sin; he also died for my pain (Isa. 53:5). I rely on him; I trust him (Chapter 7).

62. I focus on learning how to love. Jesus said this was most important (Jn. 15:9,12-13). Here all qualities of Christlikeness converge (Col. 3:12-15).

CHAPTER SEVENTEEN

With All Your Strength – Body

Your body is a temple of the Holy Spirit. You are not your own. So glorify God in your body. 1 Corinthians 6:19-20

1. In considering the five components of the human person Jesus referred to in Mark 12:29-31, we now come to strength (the body). It too must be re-formed.

2. Our body is the one component of our person that is physical. It locates us in the material creation. We are spiritual beings who have physical bodies.

3. Life in a rebellious, darkened, material world has negatively impacted my body. This in turn has affected my heart, soul, mind and personal relationships.

4. We must avoid all attitudes of body-hatred. The wrong that resides in our bodies is not the fault of our bodies. It was caused by the impact of sin upon our bodies.

5. God created the human body good (Gen. 1:31). When the second Person of the triune God came to earth, he took on a human body (Heb. 10:5).

6. In a human body, Christ:
   - bore the consequences of our sin (1 Pt. 2:24)
   - was raised from the dead (Lk. 24:39)
   - will come again (Acts 1:11)

7. How did wrong enter our bodies? A vital feature of the human body is the capacity to learn behaviors and then store them. This makes human life work.

8. Countless behaviors are stored in our bodies: how to tie our shoes, speak a language, engage in a sport, drive a car, do our job, relate to others.

9. In many cases this learning happens consciously—we have to think about it. Then it is gradually stored away and becomes habitual. We access it subconsciously.

10. Our problem: Our bodies can learn and store away habitual behaviors that are unlike God and therefore damaging to us and others.

11. "Let not sin therefore reign in your mortal body, to make you obey its passions" (Rom. 6:12). My body was not created with sin; it learned sin.

12. Sin "reigns" in my body through sinful behaviors I have learned, stored and now habitually (often subconsciously) practice. How can this "reign" be broken?

13. Three processes shape the re-forming of my body:
   - I take steps to retrain my body.
   - I trust the Holy Spirit to transform my body.
   - I honor and care for my body.

14. **I take steps to retrain my body:**
    - I unlearn destructive behaviors.
    - I replace them with behaviors I learn from Jesus.

15. "Do not present your members to sin as instruments for un-righteousness" (Rom. 6:13a). "Members" certainly includes bodily parts.

16. What if at times I simply do not have the ability to avoid presenting my members for unrighteousness? This was true even of Paul!

17. "I see in my members another law waging war against the law of my mind and making me captive to the law of sin that dwells in my members" (Rom. 7:23).

18. This points us back to some of the previous chapters we have studied. See Chapter 8: Spiritual Practices.

19. I choose spiritual practices, not to punish myself (or my body!), but to open myself to God. I learn them from Jesus and Judeo-Christian fathers and mothers.

20. An example of how spiritual practices can support the re-forming of my body is the benefits that can come by fasting from food. Jesus taught it. Jesus practiced it.

21. What benefit does voluntarily, temporarily, fasting from food have? It gives me the experience that I am not compelled to give in to every demand of my body.

22. A mega-theme in the teaching of Jesus and the apostles is that new life comes forth from death. Paul wrote that he died every day! (1 Cor. 15:31)

23. Why would anyone choose to die every day? In order to exchange what is damaged for what is new and deeply desirable. This involves the body.

24. "Always carrying in the body the death of Jesus, so that the life of Jesus may also be manifested in our bodies" (2 Cor. 4:10).

25. But the re-training of the body is certainly not all negative. A key to understanding the biblical teaching on death: death is the pathway into life.

26. **I trust the Holy Spirit to transform my body.** "Present yourselves to God" (Rom. 6:13b).

27. This is primary. We present our whole being to our Creator. We went away from him. We suffered the consequences. We now accept his invitation to return.

28. Learning how to present ourselves to God takes us back to Chapter 5: *Practicing God's Presence*. Living in God's Presence, I am transformed.

29. Presenting my whole being to God includes presenting my bodily members to God (Rom. 6:13c). This may require healing (Chapter 7).

30. Saying "No" to destructive bodily behaviors, and saying "Yes" to presenting my members to God—this is what obedience is.

31. "For if you live according to the flesh you will die, but if by the Spirit you put to death the deeds of the body, you will live" (Rom. 8:13).

32. Obedience is teamwork between heart and body. Heart decisions to obey are expressed by bodily actions, even if these actions seem hard at first.

33. Obedience is teamwork between my choices and the Spirit. I choose to learn to obey. I follow spiritual practices. I rely on God. The Spirit re-forms my body.

34. Motivation to obey grows stronger as the fruits of obedience become sweeter. The ultimate fruit: A life characterized by experiencing and sharing God's love!

35. Jesus: "If you keep my commandments, you will abide in my love, just as I have kept my Father's commandments and abide in his love" (Jn. 15:10).

36. **I honor and care for my body.** Contrary to punishing my body, I honor my Creator by honoring the body he made through rest, food, stress and medical care.

37. Rest. I am responsible to give my body the rest it needs. How much physical illness is caused by stressed-out bodies driven by chaotic souls?

38. A rested body is a vital pre-requisite for practicing God's Presence. It is hard to focus on God when I am exhausted or falling asleep.

39. Rest is central to the principle of Sabbath. God worked. Then he rested. We are to do likewise. God invites us to enter with him into rest (Heb. 4:9-11).

40. Food. I am responsible to give my body the food it needs—not too little, not too much, and the kinds of food that will nourish, strengthen and protect it.

41. Stress. I am responsible to moderate the pull of compulsive activity all around me. Much stress is inflicted on the body by a deep striving for significance.

42. Medical care. I am responsible to take the medical needs of my body seriously and make provision for their care. Denial is not a Godly response.

43. "Wretched man that I am! Who will deliver me from this body of death? Thanks be to God through Jesus Christ our Lord" (Rom. 7:24-25a).

CHAPTER EIGHTEEN

Loving Your Neighbor
(Personal Relationships)

Above all these put on love, which binds everything together in perfect harmony. Colossians 3:14

1. In considering the five components of a person in Mark 12:29-31, we come to our social self—how we relate with our neighbors. This too must be re-formed.

2. God is social. He is One, and yet he is not alone. God is relational, a community of three loving Persons—Father, Son, and Holy Spirit.

3. I am social. I am an individual, yet I am not made to be alone. I am relational, created with the capacity and need for loving personal relationships.

4. Where do I start in seeking to become more like Jesus? The process begins and ends with love. In love all ingredients of Christlikeness converge (Col. 3:14).

5. As I am gradually transformed into Christlikeness, I increasingly become the kind of person who loves. To love competently requires emotional maturity.

6. "When I was a child, I spoke like a child, I thought like a child, I reasoned like a child. When I became a man [adult] I gave up childish ways" (1 Cor. 13:11).

7. God is love. He both loves and is loved. Each person of the Trinity loves, and is loved by, the other two. God is a community of all-competent love.

8. God created me to be like him—to receive love, and then extend love to others. My need to be loved is so great that only God can fully meet the need.

9. As I receive the love I need, greater capacity grows within me to love others. Being fully and sufficiently loved gives me the resources to love my neighbor.

10. My need to be loved is so great that initially my capacity to love others is quite limited. I have been inadequately loved. We all have.

11. Inadequately loved? Whose fault is that? It's mine! I turned away from the all-competent Lover. God never stopped loving me; I stopped loving him.

12. When we distanced ourselves from God, we became un-coupled from the only Source who is able fully to satisfy our deepest longing to be loved.

13. Love my neighbor? I know people I could never love! The answer: Go deep with God. Experience his love. Watch love grow inside you.

14. What is love?
    • Love is choosing to desire my neighbor's highest good.

- Love is readiness to take appropriate action to achieve that end.

15. Love is more than emotion, though emotion is surely involved. Competent love requires discernment—what is really my neighbor's highest good?

16. Love for our children does not always translate into giving them what they want. They cannot yet fully discern what their own highest good really is.

17. I too cannot always discern what my highest good really is. So my Father protects me. It is grace that he does not always give me what I want or ask for.

18. Since love is about my highest good rather than my current desires, I can be angry and bitter toward someone who is actually loving me well.

19. When emotional wounds incurred in childhood remain unhealed, we can enter adulthood in the grip of unresolved pain leading to immature coping behaviors.

20. Thoughts may be in bondage to hurt. Unhealed pain may have trapped us in self-absorption—unable to recognize and access the Love that heals.

21. Harboring feelings of being unloved fosters resentment, anger, blame. Such emotional baggage can energize behaviors harmful to soul and body.

22. Driven by a deep need to be loved (common to us all, though we are often unaware of it, or in denial). We try to find love in ways that don't work.

23. Our need to be loved can only be satisfied in the intimacy with God for which we were created. This is the most fundamental human need.

24. Access to this love was severed when we broke with God and went our own way. Christ came to reconcile—heal and restore—the relationship.

25. Our need for love cannot be adequately met by other people. Our need is too great and they have the same need. When we look to others, needs collide.

26. Tragically, this is often the case in marriage. A relationship begins romantically (not rooted in reality). After a while, needs surface. Then needs collide.

27. Expecting others to meet my need to be loved easily degenerates into clinging and demanding. This frightens others away.

28. Many who feel lonely and abandoned are unaware that their own actions may well have contributed. Demanding that others love me is not the answer.

29. Of course I need the love of other people—we all do. How do I get it? I rely on God. I look to him alone. He brings other loving people into my life.

30. To relate well with others, I must understand the distinction between *demanding* and *requesting*. The way of love is the *request*.

31. Making demands of others dishonors them. It does not respect their freedom to make their own decisions. It is not kind.

32. Making a request of another honors that person. I accept his or her response without disapproval or blame. I trust God to work through it.

33. God's love for me develops my capacity to love my neighbor. Loving my neighbor develops my neighbor's capacity to love his neighbors.

34. God's love is the source of all love. Here is how he designed human life:
    - God loves me—I know his love experientially.
    - God's love expands my capacity to love God.
    - God's love expands my capacity to love my neighbor.
    - My love for my neighbor expands his capacity to love me and others.

35. I learn to relate to others—even spouses and family members—as if Christ were between us. My primary relationship is Christ; then through him to others.

36. When you and I relate directly, issues in you ultimately arise that irritate me. But I have only my own love-deprived resources with which to respond.

37. When Christ stands between us, his Spirit, teachings, cross, and love shape my responses. They generate patience, kindness, understanding, mercy.

38. This is crucial in understanding Christian community. Each member's primary relationship must be Christ. Christ then unites the members as one.

39. When community members look primarily to others to meet their need to be loved, relationships remain immature, man-centered, soulish, vulnerable.

40. We learn how to love others by experiencing the ways in which Christ loves us. God's love is more than a theology. It becomes my daily reality.

41. Love leads to joy, peace, and fulfillment. Non-love (anger, contempt, evil speaking, lust, greed, self-love) leads to wounding, chaos, and emptiness.

42. "As the Father has loved me, so have I loved you. Abide in my love" (Jn. 15:9). Can Jesus possibly love us that much?

43. His love teaches us how to love our neighbors. "This is my commandment, that you love one another as I have loved you" (Jn. 15:12).

44. To become like Jesus, I focus on learning how to become the kind of person who loves. All components of Christlikeness flow together in love.

45. Put on compassion, kindness, humility, meekness, patience. Bear with one another; forgive each other. Love binds these together (Col. 3:12-14).

46. Love is patient, kind; does not envy, boast; is not proud, rude; does not demand its own way; is not irritable, resentful (1 Cor. 13:4-5).

47. Love does not rejoice in evil but rejoices in truth. It bears, believes, hopes and endures all things. Love never ends (1 Cor. 13:6-8).

48. Hypocrisy is not of love. Love hates evil. It clings to what is good. Love has no desire to outdo someone; it wants to honor him (Rom. 12:9-10).

49. Love is patient when things are hard, quick to pray for others, oriented toward giving to the needy, ready to offer hospitality (Rom. 12:12-13).

50. Love blesses those who persecute us; it does not curse them. It rejoices with the rejoicing and sorrows with the sorrowing (Rom. 12:14-15).

51. Love knows how to live in harmony with others. It doesn't put on airs. It befriends the lowly. It doesn't boast in its own wisdom (Rom. 12:16).

52. Love never repays evil with evil. In every matter for which it is responsible, it seeks peace with all. Pay-back is left to God (Rom. 12:17-19).

53. Love tries to meet the genuine needs of its enemy. It rejects evil as a response. It overcomes evil with good (Rom. 12:20-21).

54. Love does these things; we don't do them by straining for more will-power. They become default settings, predictable responses, as love (Christ) forms within.

55. We "hang out" with Jesus. We see how he responds to us. His responses seep into our thoughts, emotions, choices. They shape the person we are becoming.

56. As we mature toward Christlikeness, we may find times when progress seems blocked. This may point to areas where inner healing is needed.

57. A common spiritual attack against a work of God is an attack on the love among the members. Be forewarned! Not to love is never an option.

CHAPTER NINETEEN

Sexuality

God's Gift for Physically Expressing "One-Of-A-Kind" Intimacy

1. The human person, in rebellion against his Creator, declares his autonomy: Only I will decide how I will behave, or even who I will be—I alone!

2. I can assume ultimate authority for my life. But this will have consequences. One area that will be affected is my relationship with my God-given sexuality.

3. Throughout history men and women have expressed themselves sexually in a variety of ways. The common motivation has been strong desire—emotion.

4. Choosing to allow emotion and desire to run freely may feel good at first. But such a lifestyle can turn out to be quite damaging in the long run.

5. Sexuality, expressed in ways for which it was designed, delights and fulfills. Sexuality, expressed in ways for which it was not designed,

deeply wounds.

6. What I do with my body affects my soul. Human souls are wounded by sexual violation. A wounded soul hinders my maturing.

7. Hanna and I visited an inner city church. The congregation, with love, acceptance and caring, was ministering to women trapped in the sex trade.

8. Looking into their faces, I saw a profound emptiness. It was as if their souls were being hollowed out, their human dignity drained from them.

9. One of God's purposes when he created us was to populate the earth. He chose to do this by giving each of us a gender. He created us male or female.

10. "So God created man in his own image...male and female he created them...And God said to them, 'Be fruitful and multiply...'" (Gen. 1:27-28).

11. I am not God. God is God. I do not decide what gender I will have. God—the One who created me—has decided what gender I have.

12. God intended for a man and a woman to forge a "one-of-a-kind" intimacy. This relationship was to be characterized by love— agape—the kind of love God has.

13. Jesus: "Therefore a man shall leave his father and mother and hold fast to his wife, and the two shall become one flesh" (Mk. 10:7-8a).

14. This unique intimacy was to be built on mutual and permanent commitment, caring, kindness, respect. God made provision for it to be expressed physically.

15. God created (designed) us so that the physical, sexual expression of this mutually committed intimacy would result in offspring—new people.

16. God intended that a child's first experiences outside the womb would be in an environment of mutually committed love between a father and a mother.

17. But humans, male and female, rebelled against God and the order he designed. Our hearts were filled with folly, arrogance, rebellion, darkness.

18. "For although they knew God, they did not honor him as God...they became futile in their thinking, and their foolish hearts were darkened" (Rom.1:21).

19. These are delicate issues. We don't discuss them to condemn. Jesus did not come to condemn. He came to save—to forgive, to heal, to transform.

20. Jesus: "For God did not send his Son into the world to condemn the world, but in order that the world might be saved through him" (Jn. 3:17).

21. To be "saved" requires that we face what is true. Nothing changes until it becomes what it is. Sexual acts that violate God's design deeply damage.

22. "For this reason God gave them up to dishonorable passions. For their women exchanged natural relations for those that are contrary to nature" (Rom. 1:26).

23. "And the men likewise gave up natural relations with women and were consumed with passion for one another..." (Rom. 1:27a).

24. "...men committing shameless acts with men and receiving in themselves the due penalty for their error" (Rom. 1:27b).

25. "Now the works of the flesh are evident: sexual immorality.... Those who do such things will not inherit the kingdom of God" (Gal. 5:19a,21b).

26. What I do with my body impacts my soul. Sexual immorality—of all kinds—wounds the soul. Jesus came to heal the soul. It happens in discipleship with him.

27. **How do I respond to sexual violations...**
    • That I may have committed?
    • That may have been committed against me?

28. **I tell myself the truth.** This may require an extended process. It probably will be hard work, and painful. I may need prayer and support from trusted others.

29. **I tell God the truth.** I cannot tell God the truth until I tell myself the truth. It may not feel like it but God is by my side—waiting for me, accepting me, loving me.

30. Jesus is saying: Let me carry the sin that has damaged you. It is too heavy for you. This is why I came—to be the One who bears your guilt, your pain.

31. **In prayer, I bring each sin to Christ on the cross**—the sin I may have committed, and/or the sin that may have been committed against me.

32. With the sin I have committed, I tell Jesus the truth. I lift my sin to him on the cross. I ask for his mercy, forgiveness, cleansing, healing. I practice his Presence.

33. With sin committed against me, I tell Jesus the truth. I lift the sin to him on the cross. I ask for his grace to forgive—to allow God to be the Judge of my abuser.

34. **Should I speak with one I have wronged?** Do I confess my sin and ask for forgiveness? This can be powerfully healing, but also risky. How might I proceed?

35. *In prayer I seek the Lord's guidance.* How does he want to lead me? What circumstances might he want to arrange? What might be his timing?

36. *Am I ready?* Have I told myself, and God, the truth? Have I brought my sin to the cross? Am I prepared not to justify myself but rely on God to be my Defender?

37. *Is the one I have wronged ready?* This might be traumatic for them. I ask for their permission to speak about this. I respect and honor their response.

38. I have dishonored the one I have wronged. I now want to go out of my way to treat them with utmost dignity and respect.

39. *I consider asking a mature, mutually trusted person to meet with us for wisdom and protection.* The one I have wronged must agree and trust this person.

40. *I acknowledge the wrong I have committed.* I am as transparent as I can be. This does not require many words. I speak with gentleness and humility.

41. *I ask for forgiveness.* I respect and honor the response. He or she may not be able or ready to forgive. I "request" forgiveness; I do not "demand."

42. *If forgiveness is extended, I accept it with tenderness and gratitude.* In Christ, healing has begun. The door has been opened for reconciliation.

43. **Should I speak with the one who has wronged me?** Do I seek to bring what is in darkness into the light and give healing a chance? How might I proceed?

44. *In prayer I seek guidance from the Lord.* This will be delicate communication and interaction. I want to be very careful not to cause further pain.

45. *Am I ready?* I practice God's Presence. Experiencing his love for me furthers my healing. I test my heart. Am I prepared to leave "pay back" in God's hands?

46. Words of truth, spoken in love, open the way for healing. This is not about condemnation. Christ did not come to condemn; he came to save.

47. *Is the one who has wronged me ready?* Offenders often seek protection behind a wall of denial. Only one who has erected such a wall can choose to remove it.

48. *I consider asking a mature, mutually trusted person to meet with us for wisdom and protection.* He who has wronged me must agree and trust this person.

49. *I ask the one who has wronged me for permission to speak about this.* I respect and honor the response.

50. *If the one who has wronged me responds with denial or self-justification,* I leave this with God. I don't argue. I am only responsible for my own responses.

51. *If the one who has wronged me responds by owning the truth,* then the

    ball is in my court. I have been given the opportunity to extend forgiveness.

52. Love beckons me to offer the one who has wronged me the chance to receive God's forgiveness and healing. How he or she responds is his or her responsibility.

53. **Destructive sexual behavior can become compulsive.** If I am concerned that I am in danger of addiction to sexual misconduct, I can respond by:
    • Becoming (or re-committing to live as) a disciple of Jesus (Chapter 2).
    • Re-orienting my being before God in humility (Chapter 3).
    • Allowing Jesus to teach me how to live in God's kingdom (Chapter 4).
    • Practicing God's Presence (Chapter 5).
    • Seeking God for healing (Chapter 7).
    • Undertaking spiritual practices (Chapter 8).
    • Asking the Lord to provide others to walk with me in my deliverance.

54. "...neither the sexually immoral...nor adulterers...nor men who practice homosexuality...will inherit the kingdom of God. And such were some of you. But you were washed, you were sanctified, you were justified in the name of the Lord Jesus Christ and by the Spirit of our God" (1 Cor. 6:9-11).

CHAPTER TWENTY

Learning How to Forgive

Changing the Effects of the Past on the Present and the Future

1. When we make choices that are out of touch with reality, we set ourselves up for suffering brutal collisions with reality.

2. What is reality? For starters, reality is that I am not God! If I try to take responsibility for what is God's responsibility, I will damage myself and others.

3. I am responsible for my own decisions. I am not responsible for God's decisions, and I am not responsible for other people's decisions.

4. What is reality? Reality is that God is Judge. He has not given me responsibility to judge. Jesus said, "Judge not, that you be not judged" (Mt. 7:1).

5. Reality is that I am a glorious being, created in the image of a magnificent God. My Father's love for me has no limits. Nothing can alter it.

6. Reality is also that I am a fallen being. I have been severely damaged as a result of my own wrong decisions, and the wrongness all around me.

7. As Judge, God has made a Way through whom I can be rescued from the guilt, dysfunctions and lostness caused by my wrong choices. This Way is Jesus.

8. God extends to me his offer of forgiveness. He has the authority to do this. I desperately need to be forgiven, although I could never earn forgiveness.

9. I must decide whether or not to accept God's offer. God has freedom to offer me forgiveness; I have freedom to decide how I'm going to respond.

10. God's forgiveness comes to me through Jesus. He is the only Way. I tell him the truth about my sin. In prayer I bring my sin to him on the cross.

11. I rely on Christ's cross to remove my guilt and all other effects of my sin. He bore my sin, my death. In exchange he now offers me his life (Rom. 6:23).

12. Experiencing God's forgiveness begins to awaken in me a heart to forgive my enemy. I am growing in Christlikeness—becoming the kind of person who forgives.

13. How can I become the kind of person who chooses to forgive? This doesn't just happen. It takes time and work. I have to learn and mature in the process.

14. I learn this from Jesus in discipleship to him. Here are eight things I learn from him that inform and develop my capacity to forgive my enemy:

15. **Forgiveness never denies or minimizes what is true.** It does not deny wrong; it is a choice in responding to wrong. Forgiveness opens the door to healing.

16. If I have cancer, healing requires 1) that someone tell me the truth, and 2) that I respond with appropriate actions. Denying what is true can lead to death.

17. **Forgiveness means I choose to leave "pay-back" to God.** Whether to retaliate, how much to retaliate, when to retaliate—these are God's decisions.

18. If I were to make these decisions about pay-back, I might well decide unjustly, even vindictively. Do I possess the required objectivity, insight, wisdom?

19. **Forgiveness means choosing not to assume the role of a victim.** As Jesus' follower, I am never a victim. Why? Because I have a heavenly Father!

20. Jesus teaches me to trust my Father's wisdom and goodness even when I don't understand. Choosing to do so, I find I grow toward emotional adulthood.

21. My heavenly Father is always with me, is all-powerful, knows everything, is fully just, loves me passionately and works all things for my good (Rom. 8:28).

22. Seeing myself as a victim traps me in immaturity. An emotionally mature adult has the required wisdom to respond to all of life in productive, redemptive ways.

23. "I believe that I shall look upon the goodness of the Lord in the land of the living! Wait for the Lord" (Ps. 27:13, 14a).

24. **Forgiveness cultivates God's healing in me and through me.** It is to my great benefit. Bitterness can harm me more than anything my enemy has done.

25. **Forgiveness is the best option for responding to past pain.** I cannot change the past, but I can change the effects of the past on the present and future.

26. **Forgiveness opens me to deeper insight.** It brings my thoughts, emotions and soul to peace and clarity. Forgiveness opens the way to wisdom.

27. Do I share any responsibility in the wrong that was done? What role might my own attitudes, words, or actions have played? Am I seeing the past accurately?

28. Wounded areas within may cause us to misinterpret the words or actions of another. Did I feel offense where no offense was intended?

29. Pain in a current relationship may be related to unhealed pain in a past relationship. This is known as transference. Mature love is not easily offended.

30. Often deep relational hurt between two people indicates they were once very close. Trust has been broken. Rebuilding it will take patience, kindness, mercy.

31. Putting aside anger and pay-back opens the way for relational healing with my enemy. Nobody wants to be around someone who is trying to punish them.

32. As I am healed by living in God's Presence, I become aware that I too need to be forgiven. My own need for mercy encourages me to extend mercy to another.

33. Jesus said if I am unwilling to forgive those who have wronged me

my Father will not forgive me (Mt. 6:14-15). Strong words! Powerful motivation!

34. **Forgiveness opens the way for reconciliation** in marriages, families, friendships, churches. Christ is making all things new (Rev. 21:5).

35. But I am only responsible for my own choices; I cannot demand something from another. If only one party is ready to forgive, reconciliation may have to wait.

36. **Forgiveness forms Christlikeness in me.** I was created to be like him. In God's Presence is fullness of joy (Ps. 16:11).

CHAPTER TWENTY–ONE

The Ministry of Reconciliation

Bringing Healing and Beauty to Wounded Relationships

1. God reconciles individuals—and also groups—who are separated relationally. This is just the kind of person he is. God is healing fractured humanity.

2. As we gradually mature toward Christlikeness, we become agents of reconciliation. This is just the kind of persons we are becoming.

3. We become agents of reconciliation in our relational circles— family, church fellowship, neighborhood, among various social groups, between political factions.

4. We serve to heal the wounds history has left behind which have alienated countries, cultures, religions, races, and the various Christian traditions.

5. What does the process of reconciliation look like? How does it start? Unfold? End? Its dynamics can be applied to both individuals

and groups.

6. The following steps are typically found in processes of reconciliation. Not all are found in every case, and they need not occur in this order. Use these as a guide:

7. **Step 1—We pray.** We invite Jesus into the situation. We humble ourselves before him. We ask for spiritual protection. We seek his insight and guidance.

8. **Step 2—We request the prayers of intercessors.** Hatred, bitterness, division are spiritual strongholds. Reconciliation involves spiritual battle.

9. **Step 3—We listen to each other's stories.** We seek to "hear" the pain of the other person or group with respect and empathy. We don't evaluate or judge.

10. **Step 4—We seek insight.** How have others been affected by us or by members of our group. We want to view our own history through their eyes.

11. To listen to someone else with respect and compassion is an act of love. To understand how our history has affected them is to grow in wisdom.

12. **Step 5—We tell our own stories.** We avoid defending ourselves, blaming or judging. This is not about who is right or wrong.

13. God will decide right and wrong. Surely there is enough of both to go around. This is about respectfully growing in trust, understanding, compassion.

14. **Step 6—We confess.** We acknowledge what we know to be true. Where we, or our family, culture, race, or denomination have wronged others, we say so.

15. It is appropriate for our confession to extend as far as the wrong has reached. Private wrong calls for private confession; public wrong for public confession.

16. Hanna and I have been so blessed by the actions of many Germans who are taking public steps to acknowledge the historic evils of their Nazi past.

17. All over Germany brass stones (Stolpersteine) are being laid in front of former homes of Holocaust victims giving their names and details of how they died.

18. Plaques are being placed where synagogues formerly stood, acknowledging the burning of Jewish houses of worship during the night of November 9-10, 1938.

19. All this is public telling of the truth. The subsequent effects are healing and the blessing of God. The spiritual atmosphere of a place can be changed.

20. **Step 7—We ask for forgiveness.** The request comes from our heart with full integrity. We are sensitive and respectful. This may be painful for both sides.

21. We give the other party the space they may need to decide how they will respond. They may be unable to forgive, or not yet ready. They may need time.

22. It is our choice to ask for forgiveness. It is their choice whether or not to extend forgiveness. We honor their response.

23. **Step 8—We extend forgiveness.** We feel no need to defend or justify ourselves or our group. God is Judge. We leave pay-back to him.

24. Hanna read from her book, *A Garland for Ashes*, in a public meeting in the city of Bonn. She sat down. Unexpectedly, a

German man came to the microphone.

25. "Hanna, my grandfather was a Nazi. He was an SS Officer. He killed people. He was in Chelmno the same time your parents were gassed to death."

26. "Hanna, I don't know what to do with that. I can only stand here and speak the words my grandfather never spoke. Will you forgive me?"

27. Hanna rose. She approached him. "I forgive you." They embraced. He wept. The crowd was gripped—silent. Something broke in the spiritual atmosphere.

28. Where we are unsure what is true and what is not, we wait for more clarity. Confessing and asking for forgiveness must be done in truth.

29. The reality of reconciliation is more sacred than who is right or wrong. When Jesus unites two parties, right or wrong is no longer the issue. Love is.

30. **Step 9—We practice representational repentance.** We follow Biblical examples of confession and repentance on behalf of our forefathers.

31. The psalmist confessed and asked forgiveness for the sins of contemporaries and forefathers (Ps. 106:6-7, and throughout the Psalm).

32. The prophet Daniel identified with and asked forgiveness for the sins of his contemporaries, his forefathers and his people (Dan. 9:4-19).

33. Hanna and I belong to a Christian initiative in which Catholics and Protestants are confessing and repenting over how they have wronged each other historically.

34. Catholics are acknowledging that the Reformation was a gift to the Body of Christ. Protestants are honoring their Catholic forefathers and mothers.

35. Reconciliation, rooted in Jesus' teachings and birthed in the Spirit, broadens. Catholics and Protestants are now confessing centuries of "Christian" anti-Semitism.

36. The initiative is expanding. We are now Messianic Jews, Catholics, Lutherans, Anglicans, Baptists, Pentecostals, non-denominational congregations, and others.

37. **Step 10—We bring our sins to Christ on the cross.** We do this in prayer. Where appropriate we also bring to him the sins of our forefathers and our people.

38. We tell Jesus the truth about our sins. We ask him to forgive us. His cross has power to forgive, cleanse, heal and reconcile (Eph. 2:14,16).

39. **Step 11—We seek opportunity to make restitution.** Where possible and appropriate we do so. In the case of historic wrongs there may be little we can do.

40. A heart to make restitution where possible shows the sincerity of our repentance. Symbolic acts may be appropriate and very healing. Love always is.

41. **Step 12—When two parties forgive each other, reconciliation can take place.** The kingdom of God becomes visible. All can see—God has done this!

42. If the other party is not yet ready for reconciliation, we respect their decision. We treat them kindly. We prayerfully keep the door open.

43. "Beloved, let us love one another, for love is from God, and whoever loves has been born of God and knows God...God is love" (1 Jn. 4:7-8).

44. Reconciliation is God's miracle. It is an expression of Christlikeness being formed in the inner life.

CHAPTER TWENTY-TWO

Honor Your Father and Mother

Learning God's Way in Relating to Authority

1. God is a social being. I am created in his image. I am also a social being. Through the circumstances of my birth God located me in a specific social setting.

2. My social setting includes the authority structures of family, religion, school, work, government, etc. God ordained that there be human authorities.

3. God's purpose in providing these authorities is good. They offer stability, protection, preservation of collective wisdom and integration into broader society.

4. Human authorities are established by God and serve as extensions of his authority. To live well I must learn how to relate effectively with them.

5. Of course these human authorities are not entirely as God intended them to be. Like me they have been damaged by sin. This leads to

dysfunction.

6. The effects of sin cause human authorities to malfunction in exercising their authority and cause me to malfunction in relating to their authority. Pain hits pain.

7. Parents were designed by God to be my initial human authorities. Disorders in how I relate to them can set in place disorders in how I relate to other authorities.

8. God chose my parents for me. Dishonoring them will negatively affect my relationship with God. I will be unable to trust him fully.

9. To mature toward wholeness I must be able to trust that my Heavenly Father has done well by me in all things, including his choice of my parents.

10. We must show mercy to our parents. There are no perfect people. There are no perfect parents. There are no perfect children. As a parent I too will need mercy.

11. Sometimes we can be very hard on our parents, only to discover years later that we have hurt or wronged our own children in similar ways.

12. To honor my parents does not mean I must be in denial about their imperfections. I learn to honor them in spite of imperfections—theirs and mine.

13. All human authorities are flawed. They are human! I am to honor them and respond in redemptive ways to their neediness. Jesus teaches me how.

14. In relating with authorities, I can be wounded far more by my own wrong responses to their actions than by the wrong actions themselves.

15. Responses that wound: anger, pay-back, evil speaking, rebellion. Responses that honor, protect, and heal: patience, understanding, forgive-ness, love.

16. When feeling inner pain, I may need to admit that I sometimes do not respond in Christ-like ways. I need the inner healing only Jesus can give (Chapter 7).

17. Speaking the truth in love, we are to grow up into Christ (Eph. 4:15). Immaturity speaks the truth in anger; maturity speaks the truth in love.

18. Honoring my parents does not mean I must be passive in the face of habitual, hurtful behaviors. I can honor them while establishing appropriate boundaries.

19. Wise boundaries offer me protection against the hurtful behavior of others toward me, and/or my own hurtful behavior toward others.

20. Boundaries become necessary when parents (or others) act in ways that are abusive physically, emotionally, sexually, or spiritually.

21. Establishing boundaries with parents can be sensitive, even painful. But done in Christ's way it can support maturing and healing for everyone.

22. Taking appropriate initiative to prevent abuse is an act of love. "Let love be genuine. Abhor what is evil; hold fast to what is good" (Rom. 12:9).

23. Godly boundaries combine love and truth. We face the truth about abuse, but we don't condemn. We respond with respect and love, but also with wisdom.

How Can I Understand Boundaries?

24. We often carry pain caused by past experiences, especially in personal relationships, where the underlying issues have never been resolved and healed.

25. We may be unaware of, or misunderstand, the underlying issues. Our easiest responses are to live in denial and/or to blame others.

26. Unresolved inner pain easily comes to the surface (we feel it) in specific situations. Family settings involving our parents are prime candidates.

27. When feeling unresolved pain, there is increased likelihood that we will "act it out"—express our negative emotions in words and/or actions.

28. Expressing unresolved pain easily takes the form of words and/or actions that are intended to retaliate—to "hurt back"—to blame, shame, or condemn.

29. Blaming, shaming, and condemning are hurtful to those who experience them, but also to those who express them. They only cause more pain. They don't work!

30. All this exposes the bondage sin causes. Those whose lives are ruled by unresolved pain are trapped in immaturity, unable to negotiate life effectively.

31. Christ's way is for us to be healed and released from this cycle of destructive words and behaviors. But we may need to take intermediate steps along the way.

32. In circumstances where harmful behaviors have a high likelihood of surfacing, it may be wise, perhaps for a season, to establish boundaries that offer protection.

How Do I Go About Setting Boundaries?

33. We establish boundaries by making arrangements beforehand to avoid situations where, based on past experiences, hurtful behaviors are likely to surface.

34. We respectfully tell our parents (or others) that we are choosing not to be present in such settings. We are prepared to tell them why.

35. We do not argue. We do not defend ourselves. We do not blame or condemn. We simply communicate our decision in a respectful, honoring way.

36. This does not mean we withdraw emotionally from a parent or anyone else. To "cut someone off" is not like God. God doesn't cut people off!

37. It does mean that actions in the past can affect the present. Relating to other people in hurtful ways, especially close family members, carries consequences.

38. We arrange to interact with parents, or others, in settings where the likelihood of hurtful behavior is reduced and protective ways for responding are at hand.

39. We keep our hearts affectionately open to our parents, but we act responsibly by taking steps to pre-empt hurtful behaviors—on our part as well as theirs.

Case Study #1

40. Whenever an adult son came home for a visit, his father would receive him warmly. But after 2-3 days the father would begin to express hostility.

41. The father, deeply wounded in his sense of self-worth, became jealous when the mother and sisters expressed esteem for the son.

42. The son came to realize that shorter home visits—perhaps for a meal or a 2-3 hour talk—worked fine. Hurtful behaviors took longer to surface.

43. He related well with his father by mail and phone. He respectfully shared that when in town he would stay with friends and come home for shorter visits.

Case Study #2

44. A daughter's out-of-town parents would come to visit and stay in her home for days. Their relationship was laced with hostility toward each other.

45. She told them that angry outbursts toward each other were hurtful for her and asked them to stop. But anger was so normal for them they could not recognize it.

46. So she told her parents that, from now on, rather than the parents visiting her, she and her husband would visit them. And they would stay in a nearby motel.

47. This allowed them to be with her parents, but excuse themselves politely and return to their motel when angry exchanges took over.

48. The daughter had learned to honor her parents while telling them the truth and establishing a way to remove herself from abusive behavior.

49. Anger is abusive—to those against whom it is directed, to those who express it, and to those who witness it. Nobody enjoys being around an angry person.

Case Study #3 (Other family members)

50. A brother found that his sister would erupt in anger toward him. He knew this partially stemmed from hurtful ways he had treated her in childhood.

51. He asked her for forgiveness, and received her assurance that she had forgiven him. Yet the outbursts of anger continued.

52. The brother came to realize that these events typically happened in family settings, especially when their mother was present.

53. After difficult interactions on the mother's birthday, he invited her for dinner in another city. Away from family dynamics, they shared a mutually blessed evening.

Conclusion

54. When allowed to do so, Christ heals the pain that causes dysfunctional behavior. We don't give up on people. We trust the Lord's work in them and in us.

55. We pray for our parents. We honor them. We keep the doors of respect and communication open. We give God time. He is making all things new.

CHAPTER TWENTY-THREE

New Life Comes Forth from Death

It Is No Longer I Who Live, but Christ Who Lives in Me

1. "Behold, I am making all things new" (Rev. 21:5). God is renewing creation. He has made every provision for each of us to become a new person.

2. Making something anew is not the same as making it the first time. It is a re-making. In the fullest sense, salvation is about re-creating what has been ruined.

3. What is involved in the process of re-making something?
   - The old—that which is damaged—must first be removed.
   - The new can then be formed.

4. What does the process of re-making a person look like?
   - The old life must first be removed—put to death.
   - A new life—an eternal kind of life—Christ's life—is then formed in its place.

5. What are the outcomes when a person is re-made—redeemed?

Forgive-ness of sin? Heaven when we die? Absolutely! Is that all? No! There is more—much more!

6. My sinful behavior expresses the broken, lost person I have become. Would God work forgiveness and heaven but leave character—who I really am—unaffected?

7. "As he who called you is holy, you also be holy in all your conduct, since it is written, 'You shall be holy, for I am holy'" (1 Pt. 1:15-16).

8. Being born again is not the end goal. It starts a process by which I am gradually re-formed toward becoming like Jesus on the inside. The fruit is Christ-like behavior.

9. Jesus: "The good person out of the good treasure of his heart produces good, and the evil person out of his evil treasure produces evil" (Lk. 6:45a).

10. Two megatrends guide and empower this life-process:
    • I submit to Christ as he, by his Spirit, removed what is death in me.
    • I rely on Christ as he, by his Spirit, replaces my brokenness with his beauty.

11. I do not control my re-creation. God does. But I must choose it. The Holy Spirit gradually forms new life within me as:
    • I choose to rely on God (walk by faith) in all of life.
    • I validate my decision to rely on God by obeying him.

12. "Death" here has nothing to do with self-abuse or condemnation. It is a grace-filled offer to remove the undesirable effects of wrongness within me.

13. "For one who has died has been set free from sin" (Rom. 6:7). This is a death I must choose. God will not force it on me.

14. These two processes permeate the teachings of Jesus and the apostles:
    - I allow Christ's death to work in me. I join him on the cross.
    - Christ, by his Spirit, forms new life—his resurrection life—within me.

15. Jesus: "For whoever would save his life will lose it, but whoever loses his life for my sake will find it" (Mt. 16:25).

16. Paul: "I have been crucified with Christ. It is no longer I who live, but Christ who lives in me" (Gal. 2:20).

17. These truths not only permeated the teachings of Jesus and the apostles. They lived what they taught! They chose death, knowing it was the avenue to life.

18. Paul speaking about Jesus: "He humbled himself by becoming obedient to the point of death, even death on a cross. Therefore God has highly exalted him" (Php. 2:8b-9a).

19. Paul: "We who live are always being given over to death for Jesus' sake, so the life of Jesus also may be manifested in our mortal flesh" (2 Cor. 4:11).

20. Throughout Church history Christ's followers, across Christian traditions, have taught that the path to life in God's Presence and Kingdom leads through death.

21. The well-known prayer attributed to the Roman Catholic, Francis of Assisi (c. 1181-1226), ends with these words, "It is in dying that we are born to eternal life."

22. Dietrich Bonhoeffer, the Protestant who stood against Nazi terror in his native Germany, wrote, "Whenever Christ calls us, his call leads us to death."

23. That new life emerges from death is a principle seen throughout

nature. Jesus used this reality to illustrate his teaching.

24. Jesus: "Unless a grain of wheat falls into the earth and dies, it remains alone; but if it dies, it bears much fruit" (Jn. 12:24).

What Must Die? The Self-Life!

25. Why is the choice to die unavoidable in accessing Christ's new life? Because the root from which all sin grows—self-centeredness (self-worship)—blocks the way.

26. God created us for a relationship with him of mutual agape love. We were to be central in his affections, and he was to be central in ours.

27. A scribe asked Jesus which commandment was most important. Jesus answered, "You shall love the Lord your God with all your heart" (Mk. 12:30a).

28. This would allow God to meet our every need directly, each moment, as we rely on him alone. His power, wisdom, and kindness would be fully available to us.

29. Sadly, our first parents violated this arrangement. They turned from God as the center of their affection. They installed the self-life there instead.

30. Being separated from God by their own choice removed them from the Source who alone could meet their needs. They were left relying on themselves.

31. But they were unable to meet their own needs. They slid into neediness, then further into damage, ruin, and lostness. We have each done the same thing.

32. Self-worship leads to self-reliance, self-will, self-effort. Self-worship

drives us unavoidably into the darkness and lostness of the self-life.

33. The "old man" or "natural man" of Scripture develops out of the choices, thoughts, emotions, behaviors, and relational wounds generated by self-worship.

34. We need to be saved from the self-life. It was formed as we sought fulfillment in all the wrong ways. It results in emptiness, pain, darkness—lostness.

35. "And since they did not see fit to acknowledge God, God gave them up to a debased mind to do what ought not to be done" (Rom. 1:28).

36. My ruined self-life must be put to death. This allows me to be re-formed with a new life—God's life—eternal life. I must choose it, but I don't do it—God does.

The Christian Believer Is "In Christ"

37. The process whereby the ruined self-life is put to death and replaced by God's new life takes place "in Christ"—a condition of God's design and grace.

38. By repentance and faith we turn again to God. He then sets us "in Christ". This is a mystery. We can't understand it by trying to analyze it—by living in our heads.

39. "Therefore, if anyone is in Christ, he is a new creation. The old has passed away; behold, the new has come" (2 Cor. 5:17). I just rely on God's word.

40. When God sets me "in Christ", by his grace I am given a new reality. But I am responsible to access its benefits—by daily choices to trust expressed by obedience.

41. What is meant by "in Christ"? One way to understand this: Rather than me trying to hold on to Christ, Christ is actually holding on to me.

42. What is meant by "in Christ"? This means that God has united me with Christ in his death and resurrection. When he died, I died. When he rose, I rose.

43. "For if we have been united with him in a death like his, we shall certainly be united with him in a resurrection like his" (Rom. 6:5).

44. This may seem unreal. I died to sin? It doesn't feel like it! I often fail when faced with temptation. Now I must decide not to live governed by what I feel.

45. "Consider yourselves dead to sin and alive to God in Christ Jesus" (Rom. 6:11). "Consider" means to choose to rely on this being true and to act accordingly.

46. "Do not present your members to sin...present yourselves to God...and your members to God as instruments for righteousness" (Rom. 6:13).

47. Our "members" are our bodily parts, but perhaps also our wills, thoughts, emotions. Spiritual practices assist us in presenting our members to God.

48. Accepting a truth by faith is more than giving mental assent. I make choices, take actions that are logical if the truth is indeed true. Faith without works is dead.

49. For a disciple of Christ to vacillate between yielding to the self-life or dying to it is to vacillate between unreality (yielding to self) and reality (dying to self).

50. Yielding to the self-life obstructs my formation by the Spirit into

Christlikeness. Dying to the self-life co-operates with the Spirit as he forms Christlikeness in me.

What Does This Look Like In Practice?

51. Limiting these truths to the realm of theology renders them sterile—inoperative. They must shape my choices and my actions. Some examples:

52. **I allocate time to be with God—to practice his Presence.** To do this I must say "no" to other things—even good things. I "die" to them.

53. **I choose not to demand my own way.** When my will is crossed, I lay down my reactions. I "die" to retaliation. I make space for my Father to work his will.

54. **I "die" to any desire to win over others,** to be more important, more successful, more praised. I thank my Father for the place in life he has given me.

55. **I choose to learn to be a servant.** Jesus: "If anyone would be first, he must be last of all and servant of all" (Mk. 9:35b). I "die" to any desire to be important.

56. **When wronged, I reject "pay back".** I accept God's role as Judge. I entrust my abuser to him. I "die" to anger and revenge.

57. **I choose to release ("die" to) my felt need to be in control.** I accept that it is God, not I, who is in control. I marvel in the deep peace this brings.

58. **I choose spiritual practices that train me in dying to self.** One example: Fasting teaches me that I do not need to be in bondage to my bodily appetites.

59. **In every life situation I seek to learn to love.** Love is choosing to set aside self interest in order to serve the interest of another. Jesus modeled the way.

60. This teaching must never leave us focused on death. The whole point is life. In Christ, the cross precedes the resurrection. Death is the doorway into life.

61. Christ's ways gradually mature me into life characterized by victory. Yes, there will be failures along the way. We grow toward victory, not perfection.

62. My failures offer me fresh chances to "die."
    • I admit my failure. I confess. At least once a day is not too often.
    • I repent.
    • I choose to trust God's Word that I am "in Christ."
    • I renew my decision to rely on Him in everything.

63. "That I may know him and the power of his resurrection, and may share his sufferings, becoming like him in his death" (Php. 3:10).

CHAPTER TWENTY–FOUR

Grace

God Doing for Me What I Cannot Do for Myself

Lord Jesus, I bring my sin, and the guilt and destructive behavior it has caused, to you on the cross. Thank you Lord! On the cross you made provision for my guilt to be removed, my wounds to be healed, and the power of sin in my behavior to be broken. Lead me now into the faith, expressed by obedience, which enables me to access this provision of your grace.

1. Every benefit from God available to humans comes by way of his grace. But often Christians have inadequate understandings of the nature and reach of grace.

2. Grace is not the same as mercy, although it is merciful. Mercy is a quality in relationships. Grace is more active—God's provision, empowerment, impartation.

3. "But by the grace of God I am what I am, and his grace toward me was not in vain. On the contrary, I worked harder than any of them, though it was not I, but the grace of God that is with me" (1 Cor.15:10).

4. Grace can never be earned, but God extends grace to us in response to our choices. God offers grace freely; we choose actions to access his offer.

5. God's grace is accessed through faith—a choice I make to rely on him. Only by his grace can my guilt be removed and I become justified before God.

6. "For all have sinned and fall short of the glory of God, and are justified by his grace as a gift, through the redemption that is in Christ Jesus" (Rom. 3:23-24).

7. "For by grace you have been saved through faith. And this is not your own doing; it is the gift of God, not a result of works" (Eph. 2:8-9a).

8. How do we know faith is genuine? Biblical faith is expressed by obedience. "For we are his workmanship, created in Christ Jesus for good works" (Eph. 2:10a).

9. Jesus: "If you keep my commandments, you will abide in my love, just as I have kept my Father's commandments and abide in his love"(Jn. 15:10).

10. Are the two ideas that we are justified freely by God's grace apart from works, and the Biblical call to a holy life, contradictory?

11. Are justification (removal of guilt) and holiness of life (Christlikeness within) related? How? Do we need to revisit how we have understood "salvation"?

12. In Scripture, the basic idea of "salvation" is "deliverance." It takes us back to the people of Israel, and how God delivered (saved) them from bondage in Egypt.

13. What all was involved when God delivered Israel from bondage? Certainly we could begin with him taking them out of Egypt and through the Red Sea.

14. But was that all? After Israel had crossed the Red Sea, and entered into the wilderness, was their deliverance complete?

15. Israel was formed in the wilderness, then entered and possessed the promised land by faith and obedience. These were essential to complete Israel's deliverance.

16. God was delivering (saving) Israel, not just *from* something, but *to* something.

17. What is Jesus' *project* on earth? Forgiveness of sin? Removal of guilt? Making it possible for us to go to heaven when we die? Absolutely! Is that all?

18. Jesus: "Everyone who practices sin is a slave to sin. So if the Son sets you free, you will be free indeed" (Jn. 8:34b, 36).

19. What does God think about one who self-identifies as being born-again but is still in the grip of sinful (destructive) behaviors. Is that really deliverance?

20. As a wise woman ministered to one in the grip of destructive behavior, he said, "I'm saved." She responded kindly, "I think there is some saving yet to be done."

21. What is the full meaning of biblical salvation? Did Jesus come to deliver us only from "guilt"? Or also from "sin"? Is there a distinction?

22. John the Baptist said of Jesus, "Behold, the Lamb of God, who takes away the sin of the World!" (Jn. 1:29b) Did he mean takes away "guilt" or takes away "sin"?

23. Does the Bible give any indication that deliverance from guilt and deliverance from sinful behavior might both be part of one overall process God works by grace?

24. What is Jesus' project on earth? For us to go to heaven when we die? Yes! Is that all? Much of the New Testament is not about going to heaven when we die.

25. The majority of what Jesus and the apostles taught was how Christlikeness, the righteousness (rightness) of the Kingdom, is formed in the inner life—now!

26. Jesus: "A disciple is not above his teacher, but everyone when he is fully trained will be like his teacher" (Lk. 6:40).

27. Paul: "My little children, for whom I am again in the anguish of childbirth until Christ is formed in you!" (Gal. 4:19)

28. What are the full dimensions of what God is doing on earth? "And he who was seated on the throne said, 'Behold, I am making all things new" (Rev. 21:5a).

29. God in Christ is restoring creation to the condition he intended for it originally. He gave mankind dominion over creation. Restoring humanity is primary.

30. "Therefore, if anyone is in Christ, he is a new creation. The old has passed away; behold, the new has come" (2 Cor. 5:17).

31. "For neither circumcision counts for anything, nor uncircumcision, but a new creation" (Gal. 6:15).

32. We might consider what is meant by a *new creation*. Some interpret this to be a transaction that takes place in heaven, unrelated to our daily lives on earth.

33. Do we find it credible that a holy God would design a righteousness that has no effect on rightness of life and behavior? Does that seem like the God we know?

34. When we seriously ponder Jesus' teachings, are we left with any doubt that he intended for us actually to do the things he said were best for us—obey him?

35. Jesus: "Why do you call me 'Lord, Lord,' and not do what I tell you?" (Lk. 6:46)

36. Jesus: "Everyone then who hears these words of mine and does them will be like a wise man who built his house on the rock" (Mt. 7:24).

37. How did the apostles understand these things? They are the original appointed-by-God interpreters of Jesus and his teachings.

38. Paul: "Put to death therefore what is earthly in you: sexual immorality, impurity, passion, evil desire, and covetousness, which is idolatry" (Col. 3:5).

39. Notice the command form "Put to death." In Scripture command forms point to actions we are to take. Ability to obey develops as we learn to access God's grace.

40. Paul: "...you have put off the old self with its practices and have put on the new self..." (Col. 3:9-10a). "With its practices" points us to life now.

41. All this presents us with a gigantic challenge: Our well-being—a blessed life—lies only in obeying God. And the ability to obey? In ourselves, we don't have it!

42. Readiness to obey is not necessarily the same thing as being able to obey. I may genuinely desire to obey, but find myself painfully unable.

43. So we come to perhaps the most misunderstood truth about grace: The ability to obey comes via God's grace just like forgiveness of sin and removal of guilt do.

44. Grace does not free us from responsibility for good works. Grace gives us the power for good works. Forgiveness, Christlikeness, heaven—all available via grace.

45. Outward behavior comes from somewhere—from the condition of the inner life. Christlikeness formed within ultimately finds expression in outward behavior.

46. One key to accessing God's grace is scheduling spiritual practices (Chapter 8). I learn these from Jesus and our Judeo-Christian forefathers and mothers.

47. By choosing spiritual practices:
    • I open my inner life to God.
    • He responds by working within me by his Spirit.
    This is all a gift, provided for me by his grace.

48. We move from sin and disobedience to purity and obedience as the inner life is transformed from rebellion and lostness to Christlikeness. God's grace works this.

49. Peter: "But grow in the grace and knowledge of our Lord and Savior Jesus Christ" (2 Pt. 3:18a). God is present. Grace is active. It does stuff. "Grow."

50. Paul: "The grace of our Lord Jesus Christ be with your spirit [inner life], brothers" (Gal. 6:18). God's grace, invited by faith into one's life, transforms.

51. The Christian's focus:
    • learning how to abide in Christ
    • not trying harder to obey

Knowing Jesus:
- cultivates the desire to obey
- then imparts the ability

52. "And God is able to make all grace abound to you, so that having all sufficiency in all things at all times, you may abound in every good work" (2 Cor. 9:8).

53. Without a proper understanding of the unlimited supply of grace available to us, the call to a righteous (holy) life can seem a heavy burden—unbearable.

54. So we seek to escape. We throw it off. We disregard, or try to reinterpret, the clear teachings Jesus said lead to life in all its fullness.

55. When obedience is a burden, we are functioning in our own strength. Christ formed within renders obedience desirable, dependable, increasingly spontaneous.

56. Jesus: "Come to me…I will give you rest…learn from me…you will find rest for your souls…my yoke is easy…my burden is light" (Mt. 11:28…).

57. "Now to him who is able to do far more abundantly than all that we ask or think, according to the power at work within us…" (Eph. 3:20).

58. We are speaking here of a life characterized by victory over destructive sinful behavior, not perfection. The apostle John described it this way:

59. "I am writing these things to you so that you may not sin. But if anyone does sin, we have an advocate with the Father, Jesus Christ the righteous" (1 Jn. 2:1).

60. John did not leave us wondering if he believed that followers of Jesus are actually to live godly lives of obedience:

61. "And by this we know that we have come to know him, if we keep his commandments" (1 Jn. 2:3).

62. "Whoever says he abides in him ought to walk in the same way in which he walked" (1 Jn. 2:6).

63. "The grace of the Lord Jesus Christ and the love of God and the fellowship of the Holy Spirit be with you all" (2 Cor. 13:14).

Made in the USA
Las Vegas, NV
02 May 2024

89420905R00095